ERICKA GLORIOUS MOORE

I UNDERSTAND

DISCOVER MENTAL HEALTH WELLNESS AND PEACE IN CHRIST

I Understand: Discover Mental Health Wellness and Peace in Christ

Cover and interior design by Ericka Glorious Moore
Edited by Dr. Rakisha Vinegar

ISBN: 979-8-234-05712-9
Book website: www.erickagloriousmoore.com
Email: ericka@erickagloriousmoore.com

Printed in the United States of America.

DEDICATION

I dedicate this to my Lord and Savior, Jesus Christ, who saves, heals, and restores. Even in your weakest moments, He hears you and will come down and rescue you. Thank God He came and helped me and brought me to a place of safety in my mind, body, and soul.

Psalm 18:4-6, 16-19 (NLT)
4 The ropes of death entangled me;
floods of destruction swept over me.
5 The grave wrapped its ropes around me;
death laid a trap in my path.
6 But in my distress, I cried out to the Lord;
yes, I prayed to my God for help.
He heard me from his sanctuary;
my cry to him reached his ears.
16 He reached down from heaven and rescued me;
he drew me out of deep waters.
17 He rescued me from my powerful enemies,
from those who hated me and were too strong for me.
18 They attacked me at a moment when I was in distress,
but the Lord supported me.
19 He led me to a place of safety;
he rescued me because he delights in me.

TABLE OF CONTENTS

Quick Reference Guide: When You Feel....vii

Acknowledgments....ix

Introduction....xi

PART 1: FROM BROKEN TO BREAKTHROUGH

Chapter 1
How Did I Get Here?....3

Chapter 2
Have You Come to Your End?....13

Chapter 3
Who Do You Believe?....25

Chapter 4
What Are You Thinking?....37

Chapter 5
What Are You Saying?....47

Chapter 6
What Are You Looking At?....63

PART 2: THE INNER WORK

Chapter 7
Who's in Your Inner Circle?....77

Chapter 8
Does It Really Matter? (Q-TIP)....91

Chapter 9
Courage Over Rejection....99

Chapter 10
Boundaries: Freedom in Every "No" & Power in Every "Yes"....109

Chapter 11
100 Ways to Forgive and Love....119

PART 3: WALKING IN WHOLENESS

Chapter 12
Celebrate the Wins, Celebrate You....143

Chapter 13
Give Yourself Permission....149

Chapter 14
Where Are You Going?....159

Conclusion
Hope for Change....173

Prayer of Salvation....177

Mental Health Toolbox....179

- Quick Reference Guide: When You Need Help Right Now Chapter Scriptures, Affirmations, and Prayers
- Ongoing Support Space
- Journal Exercise
- Recommended Books
- Research and Source Notes

About the Author....233

QUICK REFERENCE GUIDE: *WHEN YOU FEEL*

Sometimes you may not know where to start.
This guide will help you find the chapter that speaks to what you may be feeling right now and point you to the encouragement you need.

If you feel... → Read this:

In despair / at the end of yourself → How Did I Get Here? (Chapter 1)

Hopeless → Have You Come to Your End? (Chapter 2)

Fearful, anxious, or stressed → What Are You Thinking? (Chapter 4) and Does It Really Matter? (Q-TIP) (Chapter 8)

Overwhelmed, overcommitted, or drained → Boundaries: Freedom in Every "No" and Power in Every "Yes" (Chapter 10)

Angry, hurt, bitter, or struggling to forgive → 100 Ways to Forgive and Love (Chapter 11)

Lonely or surrounded by the wrong people → Who's in Your Inner Circle? (Chapter 7)

Rejected or feeling not good enough → Courage Over Rejection (Chapter 9)

Unworthy or struggling with self-worth → Who Do You Believe?

(Chapter 3) and Give Yourself Permission (Chapter 13)

Neglected, abandoned, or betrayed → Who Do You Believe? (Chapter 3)

Doubting God, yourself, or your future → What Are You Thinking? (Chapter 4)

Negative, critical, or defeated by your words → What Are You Saying? (Chapter 5)

Distracted or pulled away from God's best → What Are You Looking At? (Chapter 6)

Lost or unsure of your future → Where Are You Going? (Chapter 14)

Afraid of settling or afraid of success → Courage Over Rejection (Chapter 9) and Give Yourself Permission (Chapter 13)

ACKNOWLEDGMENTS

No one gets through life, healing, or purpose alone. There are so many people who loved, encouraged, prayed for, and stood by me while this book was being written.

First and foremost, I want to thank my mom, Maria Moore, for your unwavering support over the years and for encouraging me to finish this book, because you believed it would help others. Your belief in me, your famous "yes," your big smile, and your constant reminder through the Word of God to "keep going" are a big part of why this book is finally complete. Thank you for always being there.

A very big thank you to my editor and friend, Rakisha Vinegar, for jumping in to help me with this manuscript. This is our second book together, and I am so grateful for your eye to see when something can be better. Thank you for helping me through the hard parts, especially when it was difficult to talk about certain things, and for reminding me that it would be okay. I truly appreciate you.

Thank you to my cousin, Mark Alleman, for your generosity and support in helping make this book possible. I truly appreciate you.

My older brother, Leslie Moore, my older sister, Tina Parham, and my twin sister, Michelle Gonzalez, for your love, support, and for being there for me when I needed to talk things through.

To my friends, Janice Michalec, Shelle Burke, Candice Jackson, and Kim Fox-Dunigan, thank you for your prayers, encouragement, and support. It has meant so much to me.

To Alyse Martin, for being a good friend and my breath of fresh air, thank you for showing me what a free life in Christ looks like and for your encouragement. I am so thankful for you.

Thank you, Darlene Alexander, for your feedback and expertise as a Christian counselor. Your insight was truly appreciated.

To my pastors, James and Sharon Ward, thank you for encouraging me to go after my dreams and for helping me believe that what God placed in my heart mattered.

To my Insight Church family, thank you for always having my back and loving me through the years. Your support has meant more than you know.

Thank you to my sweet and kind nieces, Isabella, Abigail, Olivia, and Samantha Mae, for contributing your artwork to some of the i understand Mental Health Awareness Cards. There are lives that have been touched because of your creativity, and I am so proud of you.

Thank you to my Vision 101 girls—Suzette Lee, Gayle Fountaine-Richards, Roxanne Smith, and Sandi Bryce—for being my cheerleaders and for believing in me.

To my writer's group, LAW (League of Aspiring Writers), thank you for your invaluable feedback, critique, and suggestions. Before sharing this book, I had lost my way for a while, but you helped me reconnect with my "why" and get back on track.

And lastly, I want to thank my spiritual mom, Pastor Nancy Shannon. So much of the wisdom, growth, and truth I have learned about who I am in Christ is greatly in part because of you. Thank you for pouring into my life.

INTRODUCTION

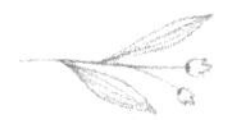

I see you, yes, you. I believe I know you.

If you picked up this book, something in you is searching.

Maybe you are having a hard time coping with life right now. Maybe you have gone through something traumatic. Maybe you feel stuck and hopeless, like there's no way out.

I decided to write this book for the millions of Christians who suffer in silence with trauma, depression, suicidal thoughts, rejection, and isolation, waiting for the day they feel safe enough to share their emotions and struggles without judgment, and to hear the words, "I understand."

Two simple words, with such deep meaning. Sometimes that is all a person needs to hear. Not opinions or condemnation. Those words have become such an anchor to my life, especially after some tough years.

If you need to hear those words right now, I tell you, "I understand." I really do. And I will also say, not in a cliché way, it will get better. No matter where you are in life.

This book is meant to encourage, bring hope, and offer peace if you feel like you are on the brink of giving up, have lost your way, have no one to turn to, and have reached one of the lowest points of your life. But there is a way out. You can have mental health wellness and peace, and you find it in Christ.

HOW THIS BOOK WAS BORN

Years ago, I created the i understand™ Mental Health Awareness Cards.

On the front: "i understand."

On the back: the suicide prevention hotline and crisis text line.

Family, loved ones, and volunteers filled the cards with words of encouragement or simple drawings meant to lift someone up in their darkest moment. Soon, those cards found their way into hospitals and mental health offices. Hundreds of lives were touched. People who felt unseen finally had a lifeline—a reminder that they were not alone.

Sometimes hope begins with two words, and a little encouragement can shift the course of someone's life.

And some of those same cards are woven throughout this book.

The voices you'll see come from people in my life, my community, and those I've met along the way here to remind you that you are not alone.

We are in this together.

HOW TO USE THIS BOOK

This book is broken into different sections for your immediate needs. As someone who has gone through crisis, I know that sometimes your mind is still enough to listen for a second at a time.

This book is intentionally structured in three parts:

PART I – FROM BROKEN TO BREAKTHROUGH

We address the internal battlefield: your thoughts, your beliefs, your words, your focus. Learn how to begin letting go of the pain that's been holding you back.

PART II – THE INNER WORK

Here, we'll dig deeper. You'll learn how to renew your mind, guard your heart, set boundaries, and forgive—practical tools that create lasting transformation.

PART III – WALKING IN WHOLENESS

Finally, you'll step into freedom. These chapters will help you dream again, celebrate progress, and give yourself permission to live the life God created you for.

Each chapter focuses on an emotion you may be facing – fear, rejection, hopelessness, lack of boundaries, loneliness – and gives you God's answer for that moment.

Inside, you'll find:

- Scriptures that bring peace and clarity
- Affirmations to strengthen your mindset
- Reflection questions to help you dig deeper
- Action steps for immediate movement
- Encouragement drawn from the original i understand Mental Health Awareness cards

Let the Holy Spirit guide you.

Read straight through if you want the full journey.

Or flip to the chapter that speaks to your present need. This book will never replace your Bible, but it should point you there—

point you to God, the only one who can truly set you free. And every section is designed to help hope rise – in you.

YOUR MENTAL HEALTH TOOLBOX

Throughout the book, you'll notice QR codes. These are part of your Mental Health Toolbox. Each code will lead you either to a video to view or additional resources at **erickagloriousmoore.com/resources**—videos, affirmations, activity sheets—tools that turn what you're reading into action.

Whenever you need a boost of hope or practical support, you can return to those resources. Think of them as me showing up to walk with you in real time.

If you take away nothing else from this introduction, let it be this: God understands, and because He understands, there is hope for you.

DISCLAIMER

I am not a mental health professional. This book is not a substitute for professional advice, diagnosis, or treatment. Always seek the guidance of a licensed professional for your mental health needs.

If you are in crisis or think you may have an emergency, call your doctor or dial 911 immediately. If you are having suicidal thoughts, call 988 (Suicide & Crisis Lifeline in the U.S.) to speak to a trained counselor anytime, day or night. If you're outside the United States, please call your local emergency line right away.

PART I

FROM BROKEN TO BREAKTHROUGH

WHERE THERE'S HOPE, THERE'S LIFE. IT FILLS US WITH FRESH COURAGE AND MAKES US STRONG AGAIN.

- Anne Frank

CHAPTER 1

HOW DID I GET HERE?

LYING IN BED IN A DIMLY LIT ROOM, STARING AT THE WINDOW in front of me. It was after midnight. The day before was supposed to be a celebration. July 4th. My niece's birthday.

But what should have been a day of happiness became one of the saddest days of my life.

With the help of a friend and my pastor, I checked myself into the hospital. She had recommended I go. I guess having a plan to end my life warranted that. It's not easy to admit—even now—but that was the reality of the situation.

I had researched methods. I calculated insurance costs so my family wouldn't be burdened. I planned passwords that my mom could access so she could handle everything.

As I lay there talking to God, one question kept rising:

How did I get here?

When did life get so heavy that giving up felt easier than holding on?

I am a Christian. Christians aren't supposed to fall apart—or so I thought. I knew how to pray. I read my Bible. I confessed the Word. I had a great support system with my family, friends, and church.

And yet I felt like life wasn't worth living.

I was embarrassed to admit I was weak.

Embarrassed to admit I needed help.

Embarrassed to admit that I couldn't fix everything, my problems or anyone else's.

As tears began to stream down my face, I heard the Lord say:

"I love you. I have always loved you. You never had to be perfect with Me. The fact that you are breathing and simply here means I love you. It doesn't matter what you do—I will always love you."

I began to cry even harder. Not because everything was fixed, but because for the first time in a long time, I felt seen.

WHEN DID IT ALL START?

Crisis rarely begins in a single moment. It accumulates.

On September 23, 2013, I lost my nine-year-old nephew, Benjamin. We called him Benny for short. His passing was sudden and completely unexpected. Benny was one of my sister's children, and at the time, they were at my parents' house.

Benny had some health challenges, mainly breathing issues related to asthma. When he struggled to breathe, he would use a breathing treatment with a nebulizer to help open his airways and improve his oxygen levels.

That night, Benny woke up screaming that he couldn't breathe. My sister immediately gave him a breathing treatment, but he kept crying out that he still couldn't breathe. She told him to relax because sometimes he struggled even with the treatment. But this time, it wasn't working.

Within moments, everything changed. His eyes rolled back, and all the color drained from his skin. My mom took him and began to give him CPR until the paramedics arrived.

Sad to say, he never made it to school the next day.

Grief does not arrive quietly. It invades.

The next two years were rough, but I felt like I was finally getting my life back on track.

Then, on January 8, 2015, I lost my older sister, Tonya, in a fatal car crash.

A snowy Chicago day, a sudden phone call from a good friend, asking me for my address.

I said, "You know where I live."

She didn't laugh. She stayed serious on the phone.

I gave her my address anyway. She said she was coming over.

About ten minutes later, I heard the buzzer to my apartment. I buzzed her in, and I saw two police officers walking behind her.

I said, still smiling, "Hey, you didn't tell me you were bringing people with you." I was in comfy clothes, not ready for company, so I rushed to throw on a robe.

My friend walked in with the two officers. One of them pulled out my sister's driver's license and asked, "Is this your sister?" I said, "Yes."

He said, "I have some news for you. Your sister was in an accident." I said, "Okay."

Then he said, "And she didn't make it."

Those words didn't fully register; they hit me all at once.

My sister and I were very close. We talked almost every day. Hearing that...didn't feel real.

Then he added, "You need to hurry to see her before we take her body to the morgue."

My friend looked heartbroken. Everything suddenly felt urgent.

I had to think fast.

I had to call my parents.

That was one of the hardest phone calls I have ever made in my life.

The screams on the other end...still echo in my memory.

It's a sound I wouldn't wish on anyone.

I had to say the words out loud: Tonya was dead.

I threw on whatever clothes I could find, grabbed a baseball cap, and my friend drove me to the hospital.

On the way, I still had to call my siblings. Over and over, I called, until one by one, they answered.

Then we came to a street blocked by a police car. I jumped out of the car, crying hysterically, and said, "My sister died, and I need to get to the hospital."

The officer let us through and told us to explain to the next officer down the street.

But a little farther ahead...I realized where we were.

We were at the accident scene.

My sister's accident.

Her car – it looked like a convertible. They had used the jaws of life to get her out.

I saw the glass, the wreckage—everything.

A female officer started yelling, telling us we shouldn't be there. My friend tried to explain.

I couldn't. I was crying so hard I could barely speak.

A couple of weeks after the funeral, I returned to work—only to lose my job of nearly six years.

I was suddenly jobless.

Then I ended a relationship with a man who wanted to marry me.

Life was hard, and emotionally, I was unraveling. Grief had layered on top of grief, and to say my life was unbalanced is an understatement.

A couple of months later, I started a new job on my sister Tonya's birthday. I felt like it was a sign from God that things were looking up.

But that only lasted for a moment.

The new job slowly revealed itself as toxic.

A workplace bully.

Exhaustion.

Financial strain.

My job schedule consumed my life. At one point, I could not see my family, who lived only ten minutes away, for a month!

Money was tight.

Dread began to fill my mornings.

And eventually, thoughts of ending my life began to take over. Deep in the trenches of life, the stress became unbearable.

Is it unbearable for you?

Do you wake up dreading the day and wanting it to be over?

For me, life had become one long stretch of pain, hurt, fear, and torment—and I wanted out.

I remember telling God that if this was all there was to life, I didn't want it.

I felt alone. I felt like no one understood. But that wasn't actually true. Even when I couldn't feel it, God had not left me.

Also, others were facing the same things I faced. Scripture says in 1 Peter 5:9 that our brothers and sisters in Christ are experiencing these same kinds of sufferings.

I once saw a quote that said, "God meets you where you are, not where you pretend to be," and that's exactly what God wants from us.

God meets you where you are, not where you pretend to be.

One of my favorite scriptures is Psalm 51:6. It says that God desires honesty in our inmost being so He can teach us to be wise.

That should be a freeing thought, because it shows He meets you right where you are.

Also, how can you ask God for help if you don't first acknowledge that you need it?

Jesus had times of pain and had no problem showing His emotions—the Bible says, "Jesus wept." (John 11:35)

In Psalms, we see David cry out in his distress as Saul tried to kill him (1 Samuel 19:1–7).

He didn't need to pretend with God. God just wanted him to be real.

And God promises us a way of escape (1 Corinthians 10:13).

At the time, I did not know what that way of escape would look like. I did not know it would be a painful, then hopeful, winding road.

But I now know this:

Rock bottom can become the birthplace of rising.

HOPE ARISE – THE FIRST GLIMMER

Ah, I remember this day. It had been over a year since my sister passed away. I was in therapy, finally starting to come to terms with the loss of my older sister.

And something unexpected happened.

Not fireworks.

Not a dramatic breakthrough.

A feeling.

I began to experience a feeling that had escaped me for some time, and when it appeared, it felt like a scene from a movie. The clouds pulled back, and the sun rays shot through—it was the word "Hope."

I could feel the warmth of the sun, but more importantly, my heart was beginning to feel again.

It brought such comfort.

And with a deep breath in, life seemed like it was going to be okay. I told my therapist, "Wow, I feel Hope."

Such a familiar friend when "it" appeared. I embraced the feeling and rested in it.

She told me I was like a caterpillar turning into a butterfly, emerging from darkness into calm.

Oh, I snuggled into it like a cozy, warm blanket. I felt so light and free—something I had longed for was finally here. I didn't know it then, but that therapy session was not just healing. It was the first time hope began to rise.

On the drive home, lyrics began forming in my mind, and I started singing.

Struggled to find who I thought I was,

Compared my life to those around me.

Found validation in those I loved,

but so lonely inside, and oh, I cried, I cried...

I wanna be free! To be all God has made me.

I wanna be free! To live my life in victory.

For the first time in a long time, I cried tears of joy.

I wasn't fixed. My life wasn't perfect. But something had shifted. I was free, at least in my mind, from the torment of believing nothing would change.

Hope had cracked the surface.

THE BEGINNING OF THE JOURNEY

If you are feeling down, depressed, worried, or afraid, stay with me.

There is a way out.

And here is what I want you to remember before we move forward:

His name is **El Roi** — the God who sees.

Long before anyone noticed your pain, He saw it. Before you found the words to explain what you were feeling, He already knew.

> ***His name is El Roi —the God who sees.***

There was someone in Scripture who discovered this truth at her breaking point — a woman who felt forgotten, overlooked, and alone... until she realized she was fully seen by God.

In the next chapter, we will find out how she came to her end and discover how hope rose in her story.

Because if it rose for her...

And it rose for me...

It can rise for you.

But before you turn the page, pause here for a moment and let these truths settle into your heart:

- I am changing — even if it feels slow.
- I am never alone.
- I am accepted in the Beloved.
- God is not finished with my story.
- Hope is not gone; it is rising in me again.

REFLECTION QUESTIONS

1. When was the last time you felt like you couldn't handle life on your own? What helped you through?
2. Read 1 Peter 5:9. How does knowing others experience similar struggles comfort you?
3. What is one step you can take today to invite hope into your situation?
4. Reflect on Genesis 16:13 — where have you experienced God as El Roi, the God who sees you?

LET GOD HAVE YOUR LIFE;
HE CAN DO MORE WITH IT
THAN YOU CAN.

- D.L. Moody

CHAPTER 2

HAVE YOU COME TO YOUR END?

WHAT HAPPENS WHEN YOU REACH THE PLACE WHERE your strength runs out?

What happens when hope feels fragile, and life still feels heavy? I know that place.

And so does a woman in the Bible whose story has stayed with me for years.

She knew what it felt like to run out of options.

She had tried everything.

She spent everything.

She endured twelve long years of suffering. And still – she wasn't better. She was worse.

Her story reminds us where real healing begins.

Let me tell you about her.

It is the woman with the issue of blood. Her story, found in Mark 5:25-34, is a powerful reminder of where true healing comes from. Imagine suffering from a constant hemorrhage for twelve years. Ladies, that's unimaginable!

And maybe that's why her story feels so familiar. Because sometimes we aren't just tired, we're tired of trying.

And here's what I began to see in her story. The first one is this:

suffering often lasts longer when we keep trying to fix things in our own strength.

Did she need to suffer that long? Was Jesus not already the healer before she encountered Him?

The answer is no.

Her healing wasn't delayed because God was absent. It was delayed because she was still searching everywhere else.

Mark 5:26 tells us:

"She had suffered a great deal under the care of many doctors and had spent all she had, yet instead of getting better, she grew worse."

Think about this in a modern context. She tried everything she knew to do.

Maybe she listened to voices promising quick solutions. Maybe she filled her days with distractions just to quiet the pain.

And still, nothing changed.

She remained trapped in the very thing she longed to escape.

Sound familiar?

Sometimes we do everything except the one thing that brings true freedom. We search for relief but never fully surrender to God. We look for answers everywhere except the place where lasting healing begins.

And that's where many of us live — exhausted from trying, yet unsure why nothing shifts.

Stories like this are not only found in Scripture. They still happen today.

AT THE END OF YOURSELF

One woman whose story reflects this so clearly is Real Talk Kim, whose real name is Kimberly Jones.

Before she ever stood on stages or encouraged others, her life had reached a breaking point.

> ***Sometimes the place where everything falls apart is the exact place where God begins putting things back together.***

She has shared openly that she had gone through three divorces. After that level of heartbreak, she began asking a hard question:

Why do people keep leaving me?

Instead of blaming everyone else, she chose to look inward.

She committed to intense counseling and began doing the deep, internal work—unpacking years of pain, facing wounds she had ignored, forgiving those who hurt her, and releasing the bitterness she had carried.

For years, she thought her story had been wasted time. But God used every painful chapter to prepare her for her purpose.

Her story reminds us of something powerful:

Sometimes the place where everything falls apart is the exact place where God begins putting things back together.

And sometimes what feels delayed...is actually preparation.

So, if you feel behind, if you feel like you've wasted years, God still has a plan for you.

Because the turning point often comes when we finally reach the end of ourselves and fully surrender to Him.

And that surrender is where hope begins again.

Real Talk Kim had her turning point.

But let's go back to the woman with the issue of blood, because she had one too.

A TURNING POINT

Mark 5:27 says,

"She had heard the reports about Jesus and came up behind Him in the crowd and touched His garment."

Everything changed the moment she heard about Jesus.

Not when she saw. Not when she felt better. Not when circumstances improved. When she heard. Something inside her began to change before anything changed outside her.

After years of suffering and searching, she realized that what her own efforts could never produce, Jesus could.

Before her body changed, her thinking changed.

Her strength had failed her. Her resources had failed her.

She heard the truth. And then, she believed the truth.

And that's where hope begins to rise, when God's Word moves from your ears into your heart.

Like her, many Christians sit in church week after week, hearing about God's power but not fully believing or living in the fullness of His promises. But hearing and believing are not the same thing.

This woman heard about Jesus and His miracles, and something inside her finally said:

He is the answer.

And that decision changed everything.

Because there is always a way that seems right to us.

Proverbs 14:12 (NLT) warns us:

"There is a way that appears to be right, but in the end, it leads to death." The only true path to healing is through Jesus Christ.

She had followed what seemed right. Doctors. Opinions. Human solutions.

But there is only one true way to life.

Jesus said it plainly in John 14:6:

"I am the way and the truth and the life. No one comes to the Father except through Me."

Not a way. Not one of many options.

The Way.

And when she believed that her thinking began to change.

Mark 5:28 reveals the moment hope took form:

"For she said, 'If I touch even His garments, I will be made well.'"

Notice what happened. She stopped rehearsing her pain. She stopped rehearsing her disappointment. She started rehearsing the possibility.

"If I touch Him...I will be healed."

That was not wishful thinking. That was faith.

Her faith moved from passively hoping to intentionally declaring.

And here's what's powerful:

Before her body changed, her thinking changed.

Before the bleeding stopped, her belief took root.

Before the miracle manifested, her faith for healing grew and hope rose.

Faith is hope for change. That is how faith works.

It believes inside before anything looks different outside.

HOW DO WE "TOUCH" JESUS TODAY?

We may not physically reach for His garment.

But we touch Him the same way she did.

Through faith.

Through belief.

Through agreement.

We touch Him when we align our words with His promises.

We touch Him when we speak His Word back to Him.

We touch Him when we speak His Word back to Him.

We touch Him when we declare truth over our feelings.

She said, "If I touch Him, I will be healed."

She spoke what she believed.

And what she believed...moved her. Because faith doesn't stay silent. It speaks.

Psalm 107:2 says: "Let the redeemed of the Lord say so."

And you could even say it this way—let the redeemed of the *Word* say so—because God's Word is what transforms us, and what transforms us should come out of us.

Not out of pressure, but out of trust. It comes into agreement with what God has already said. Because words reveal belief. And belief releases faith.

SEEKING GOD LEADS TO FINDING HIM

This woman did not wait for Jesus to find her.

She went after Him.

She pushed through the crowd. Through shame. Through rejection. Through fear.

Twelve years of isolation could have made her shrink back. Instead, desperation fueled determination.

And that's what faith often looks like, pushing through what stands in your way.

You may not be fighting through a physical crowd. But maybe you're fighting through:

Doubt.

Disappointment.

Fear.

Exhaustion.

Lies.

And yet the promise still stands.

James 4:8 says:

"Come near to God and He will come near to you."

He does not move away from you in your weakness.

Even when we feel overwhelmed. Even when you feel unworthy. Even when you feel unseen.

Hope rises when you move toward Him.

FAITH PLEASES GOD

Hebrews 11:6 reminds us:

"And without faith it is impossible to please God, because anyone who comes to Him must believe that He exists and that He rewards those who earnestly seek Him."

Faith connects us to His power.

And the moment she acted, everything shifted.

Mark 5:29 (AMPC) says,

"And immediately her flow of blood dried up at the source, and she felt in her body that she was healed of her distressing ailment."

Immediately.

Twelve years ended in one act of faith.

Not because she was perfect.

Not because she deserved it.

Not because she had everything figured out.

Faith always stands out.

But because she believed.

And Jesus stopped.

Mark 5:30 says, "At once Jesus realized that power had gone out from Him. He turned around in the crowd and asked, 'Who touched My clothes?'"

Imagine that moment.

In a crowd of people pressing around Him...One touch stood out.

And then He said, "Daughter, your faith has healed you. Go in peace and be freed from your suffering."

Faith always stands out.

TAKEAWAY – WHERE HOPE RISES

Maybe your situation may seem impossible. Maybe you feel like you've tried everything. Maybe you've spent emotional energy, mental strength, and spiritual effort, and nothing feels different.

But what if this is not the end?

What if this is the turning point?

When you come to the end of yourself, you come to the beginning of surrender.

Driven by desperation, she pushed through the crowd—through fear, shame, and uncertainty. Humbled, she believed that touching Jesus' garment would heal her. And in her brokenness, she acted in faith—and she was healed.

He is the Alpha and the Omega. The first and the final word. The beginning and the end.

And when His Word becomes the loudest voice in your life, freedom begins.

If you are struggling with something that's burdened you for years—a diagnosis, trauma, or a lie you've believed—let God reign supreme over those thoughts.

> ***When His Word becomes the loudest voice in your life, freedom begins.***

Surrender it to Him. Bring it to Him. Because hope does not rise in self-reliance. Hope rises in surrender.

MY STORY IN HERS

Reading her story, I saw myself.

I had tried my own ways. I had done what I knew to do. And still,

I found myself tired, worn down, and at the end of my rope.

It started with admitting I needed help. It started with realizing I couldn't fix everything on my own. With choosing to reach for God instead of reaching for another solution or false comfort—TV, social media, phone calls, and anything else that distracted me from what I was really feeling.

I didn't know it then, but that was the beginning of something new. Not the end of my story, just the end of doing life my way.

But somewhere in that place, the moment I stopped trying to control everything—right at the end of myself—hope began to show up again.

REFLECTION QUESTIONS

Take a moment. Sit with these.

1. What area of your life do you need to stop handling in your own strength and fully surrender to God?
2. What "crowd" are you facing right now — fear, doubt, distraction, pride — that you need to press through?
3. What is one faith declaration you can begin speaking daily, like the woman who said, "If I touch Him, I will be healed"?
4. How would your life change if you truly believed the authority Jesus has given you?
5. What step of surrender can you take today that allows hope to rise again?

WHOEVER HAS YOUR EAR,
HAS YOUR LIFE.

- Terri Savelle Foy

CHAPTER 3

WHO DO YOU BELIEVE?

IN THE LAST CHAPTER, WE SAW WHAT HAPPENS WHEN you reach the end of yourself—when you finally decide to reach for Jesus.

When I was coming out of one of the darkest seasons of my life—walking through my mental health journey and slowly climbing out of the pit I had fallen into—something became painfully clear:

I had believed the wrong voices.

Not intentionally.

Not maliciously.

But over time, I had allowed lies to shape my identity.

I didn't realize how much authority God had already given me.

And I didn't realize how much what I believed was affecting how I lived.

During that season, I felt powerless, overwhelmed, and defeated. It felt like life was dictating my path.

Hopelessness crept in, along with fear, envy, and comparison. I believed the lie that my life was over... that I had missed my chance.

That is never the end of the story.

Jesus already paid for every broken piece, every mistake, every failure, every moment we thought disqualified us.

Freedom was always available.

I just had to believe it.

THE LIES WE BELIEVE

One of the biggest lies I believed was this:

I am damaged goods. I thought I was too broken to start again. Maybe you've heard those voices too:

"It's too late."

"You missed your window."

"You should be farther along by now."

Those words became strongholds in my mind.

I took my eyes off Jesus and placed them on people, on my career, on circumstances.

Success became identity.

Failure became identity.

And slowly, I forgot who I really was.

WHEN ONE LABEL CHANGED EVERYTHING

I once worked with a young man, just nineteen, who shared his lifelong dream of joining the army. He had wanted to serve since he was a child. But something had blocked him. A label.

As a child, he had gone through trauma and depression and received counseling. During that time, he was given a mental health diagnosis. Though he had healed and moved forward, the label stayed on his record.

The military rejected his application, not because of who he was now, but because of who he once was.

I asked him, "Can that be removed from your record?"

He said, "No. That label follows me for life."

His parents may have made that decision to allow the therapist to put it on his records with good intentions, never realizing it would later cost him his dream.

And in that moment, something became clear to me:

We have to be careful what we call people, and what we allow ourselves to be called.

THE VICTIM LABEL

During this season in my life, everything felt heavy.

I felt like a victim.

It felt justified.

I would look around and think:

Why does it seem like everyone else is doing well...and I'm not?

Why does it feel like my family is getting hit so hard, and everyone else's life seems perfect?

Why do we keep going through hard times? What did we do to deserve this?

Without realizing it, I had started agreeing with a quiet belief:

Life is happening to me.

And the more I believed that, the more powerless I felt.

But God didn't leave me there.

Through what I learned in my pastor's book, Zero Victim, by

James Ward, I began to see something clearly.

He defines victim thinking like this:

Victim thinking keeps you stuck in your past with no forward progress. Even though your past explains who you are, it should not define who you are.

That hit me.

He teaches that a victim mindset will keep you stuck until you decide to live victoriously. And through the work the Holy Spirit was doing in me, something started to change.

The Holy Spirit said to me, "You can be pitiful, or you can be powerful, but you can't be both."

That was a hard truth—but it was a freeing one.

Because if I wanted to stay in a place where I was always justified, always pitied, and always stuck, I would never change.

Victim thinking keeps you stuck in your past with no forward progress.

But if I wanted to grow, I had to choose who I would be.

Empathy may comfort you, but only the truth of God's Word can change you.

I started to see that while I could not control everything happening around me, I could choose how I responded.

I did not have to build my identity around what happened to me.

I was not a victim.

And I was still called.

Still chosen.

Still loved.

Still capable of moving forward.

And that change did not come from willpower.

It came from yielding to the Holy Spirit and choosing God's way over my feelings.

And when I finally surrendered what I was feeling to God, He began to show me who I already was in Him.

CHOOSING THE TRUTH

Another woman who had to decide what she would believe is Christine Caine.

When she obtained her birth records as an adult, she discovered painful labels attached to the beginning of her life:

"Unwanted."

"Illegitimate."

Words that could have shaped her identity for the rest of her life.

But she had a choice.

She could believe what was written about her—or she could believe what God said about her.

"I had to choose which of these documents I would entrust with my life."

— Christine Caine, Undaunted

And that is exactly what she did.

She chose truth over labels.

Chosen.

Loved.

Called.

Her story is a reminder that the labels placed on you do not have to become the identity you live by.

The question is not what has been said about you—

The question is: what do you believe?

GOD USES IMPERFECT PEOPLE

Did you ever feel like you had to be perfect before God could use you? Like you needed one more degree, one more credential, or one more level of confidence before stepping into purpose? I used to think that way.

But here's what God says.

In 2 Corinthians 3:4–5:

"We are confident of all this because of our great trust in God through Christ. It is not that we think we are qualified to do anything on our own. Our confidence comes from God."

We are not qualified on our own.

Our confidence comes from looking to God and trusting in Him.

We can't do it on our own—but with His help, we are made confident.

Seeing that I didn't need to be perfect brought me so much comfort.

Because my story was never meant to be for perfect people.

And neither is yours.

It was for the broken.

The overlooked.

The ones who feel disqualified.

Because God has always used imperfect people.

Look at Scripture:

- Jacob was a cheater
- Peter had a temper
- David had an affair
- Noah got drunk
- Martha was a worrier
- Jonah ran from God
- Paul was a murderer
- Gideon was insecure
- Miriam was a gossip
- Thomas was a doubter
- Sarah was impatient
- Elijah was moody
- Moses stuttered
- Abraham lied
- Lazarus was dead
- Rahab was a prostitute
- Ruth was a Moabite
- Solomon was a womanizer
- Jeremiah was depressed

And still — God used them.

A favorite quote I heard from Mark Hankins: "God has a reputation of working with some real losers and making them champions!"

Without Christ, none of us has anything to brag about. It doesn't matter if you have success by the world's standards—great job, house, kids, money—without God, you're still empty. Because when you pass away, none of that comes with you.

God will ask: What did you do with what I gave you? How did you use it for My glory?

We were made for fellowship with God, to use our possessions to bless others and further God's Kingdom.

You have never gone too far to come back.

Proverbs 24:16 reminds us:

"The godly may trip seven times, but they will get up again..."

And God is so rich in mercy. His mercies are new every morning (Lamentations 3:23).

And we are never alone.

We also have the Holy Spirit to help us on this journey. Jesus said He should leave so the Holy Spirit would come (John 16:7). He is our guide, counselor, comforter, wisdom, friend, direction, and guidance.

WHO DO YOU BELIEVE?

At the end of the day, everything in your life is the result of who you have believed.

Do you believe God?

Or your circumstances?

Friends?

Traditions?

Feelings?

Your fears?

Your past?

Because whatever has your agreement... has your direction.

And when you finally agree with God, something shifts.

Peace begins to rise.

Hope begins to return.

And just like we saw in Chapter 2, breakthrough begins when you stop agreeing with everything else—and you finally agree with Jesus and what He says, which is the Word.

What you believe shapes what you think.

What you believe shapes what you think.

And what you think shapes the life you live.

WELLNESS CORNER: ACTION STEPS

- Take 10 minutes to think about all that you have overcome in your life up to this point.
- Who helped you to get there? How did you feel when you overcame in that area?
- Did God help you more than once in this area?

PRAYER

God,

I surrender my life to only You. Your voice, Your way, Your peace—You are my source. You alone. I don't need to seek anything other than You to supply all my needs. Thank You for always being there for me and leading me even though I haven't always recognized it. Thank You for Your faithfulness.

REFLECTION QUESTIONS

1. What lies have you believed about yourself that God is calling you to replace with His truth?
2. How has God shown His mercy in your life, even when you've fallen?
3. Which biblical example of an imperfect person encourages you the most?
4. Where do you need to rely on the Holy Spirit instead of your own strength?
5. What step will you take this week to "push through the crowd" and reach for Jesus?

BEFORE YOU CAN CHANGE YOUR THINKING, YOU HAVE TO CHANGE WHAT GOES INTO YOUR MIND.

- Zig Ziglar

CHAPTER 4

WHAT ARE YOU THINKING?

EVERY BELIEF HAS A STARTING POINT. AND THAT starting point is the mind. Long before your life shifts outwardly, something must change within your thinking. That's where the real battle begins.

THOUGHT FLOOD: YOU HAVE THE POWER TO CHOOSE

Every single day, your mind is flooded with thoughts—around 70,000 of them! Imagine a text popping up every second. The problem? Most of those are repeats from yesterday, and many are negative.

But here's the truth that changed my life: you do not have to believe every thought that crosses your mind.

We may not control what comes at us, but we are responsible for how we respond to it.

Luke 10:19 reminds us that we have authority—even over our thoughts.

When fear tries to creep in, we can choose faith. When comparison tries to steal our peace, we can declare our worth in Christ.

THE POWER OF A THOUGHT

"Your life is headed in the direction of your most dominant thoughts." — Earl Nightingale

As believers, our thoughts can either make us or break us. We can live a life of freedom and joy, or one filled with fear and regret. It all starts with what we allow into our minds.

A person's life is built on a series of thoughts.

A person's life is built on a series of thoughts. A father tells his son, "You will never amount to anything." The son believes it. And slowly, he lives it out. One thought can shape an entire future.

Our lives today are the result of the thoughts we agreed with yesterday, good or bad. That's why Scripture constantly calls us to guard our hearts and renew our minds.

CHOOSE LIFE

Deuteronomy 30:19 says:

"Choose this day who you will serve... life or death, blessings or curses."

God doesn't hide the answer.

He makes it clear: Choose life. Choose His way of thinking. Why? Because when we do, we tap into blessings, peace, and prosperity.

What blew my mind is the verse right before that—Deuteronomy 30:15. It lays it out even more clearly: "See, I set before you today life and prosperity, death and destruction."

That means every day, with every thought and every response, we are choosing between a mindset that leads to life or one that leads to disaster.

I was recently at a wedding for a dear friend, and right before the big moment—the kiss—the pastor said, "With the power vested in me, I now pronounce you husband and wife. You may now kiss the bride."

And immediately I thought:

What power has been vested in us through Christ?

We have authority.

Authority to shift our thoughts.

Authority to speak life.

Authority to rewrite the story the enemy tried to write.

When we walk in righteousness, that is the "right way" of doing things.

God isn't confusing us.

He's saying:

"Choose My way. It leads to life."

And yet so many believers are struggling, stuck, and defeated. Why? Because without realizing it, we keep agreeing with our feelings, circumstances, unforgiveness, etc.

Joyce Meyer said that when we walk in righteousness, that is the "right way" of doing things. And righteousness isn't just about moral behavior—it's about thinking God's way, seeing ourselves the way He sees us, and choosing the path He laid out.

Joshua 1:8 gives us the blueprint. Meditate on God's Word. See yourself according to it. Then you will be prosperous and have good success.

We have to first get the image on the inside to match what we say we want on the outside. We don't have to struggle through this life. We can begin to live a successful life when we meditate on God's Word.

THE STUDY THAT CHANGED EVERYTHING

A study by the Center for Bible Engagement surveyed over 100,000 people across multiple countries between the ages of 8 to 80.

The results were profound: the key to transformation wasn't prayer, church attendance, or small groups. The tipping point was consistent Bible engagement—specifically, reading God's Word at least four times per week.

When participants read Scripture four or more days a week, discouragement dropped by 31%, bitterness in relationships by 40%, anger by 32%, and feelings of loneliness by 30%. Struggles with destructive thoughts fell by 32%, and difficulty forgiving others decreased by 31%.

Our mindset won't shift until our minds are consistently renewed.

But reading only once or twice a week didn't move the needle. Their struggles were just as high as those who didn't read the Bible at all. The takeaway? Our mindset won't shift until our minds are consistently renewed.

Even better, the study revealed that those who read four or more times per week were 228% more likely to share their faith, 231% more likely to disciple others, 407% more likely to memorize Scripture, 416% more likely to give to their church, and 218% more likely to support other causes. That's transformation in action!

PAIN OR PLEASURE: IT'S STILL A CHOICE

If you are ready to move forward, you have to recognize what's been driving your choices. Tony Robbins says that two things drive us in life: pain and pleasure. We are either trying to get away from the pain that our thoughts have created, or we are enjoying pleasure and want to hold onto it. Either way, the direction we go in life is based on what we think.

How do we begin to shift? It starts with one decision: take back your mind. So, if you look around and don't like what you see, guess what? You can change it. It starts with a decision to move forward and never look back.

IMAGINATION: A HOLY GIFT

When was the last time you used your imagination for something good? Many of us use it to worry, rehearse trauma, or prepare for rejection. But God gave us our imagination as a tool to see the future He promised.

When you start seeing yourself as healed, restored, joyful, and confident, your brain begins to adjust. You walk differently. You speak differently. This is not pretending—this is you agreeing with God's thoughts.

When my life was falling apart, it started in my mind. Poor decisions, shame, and a false belief that I wasn't worthy of God's love began to pile up. I locked my heart away to protect myself, but by doing so, I also shut out God.

The root of it all? One thought: rejection. That single lie led to a cascade of choices that shaped my life. But God, in His grace, met me there and reminded me: I have the mind of Christ. I can choose new thoughts. I can believe what He says about me.

THE TRUTH ABOUT THOUGHTS AND FEELINGS

Dr. Caroline Leaf, a cognitive neuroscientist, found that 75–98% of mental, physical, and behavioral illness comes from our thought life. Only 2–25% is linked to the environment and genetics.

That means our thoughts matter. Toxic thoughts produce toxic emotions, which create toxic attitudes and behaviors. But the good news? Your brain can heal. You can rewire toxic thought patterns and create new, healthy ones.

When we intentionally direct our thoughts, we improve brain function by 35–75%. God designed your brain to respond to faith, hope, and love. You are not a victim of your thoughts. You are the architect of your mindset.

Neuroscience calls this ability to change the brain *neuroplasticity*—the brain's God-designed ability to create new neural pathways when we practice new thoughts, habits, and beliefs. Isn't that powerful? What God said in Romans 12:2 about being *"transformed by the renewing of your mind"* is exactly what scientists now confirm.

You can rewire toxic thought patterns and create new, healthy ones.

Dr. Caroline Leaf teaches that when we intentionally focus on a new thought—like a Scripture or a truth about God—and rehearse it daily, we begin to rewire our brain. If we repeat that truth for 21 days, we begin to form a new pathway. If we do it for three cycles (about 63 days total), it becomes a permanent, automatic way of thinking. That means you're not just learning—you're transforming. You're literally creating a new mind.

RENEWING YOUR MIND DAILY

My freedom came because I reached a point when I finally believed what God said about me, instead of how I felt about myself. So, to do this, I had to learn to replace my thoughts with God's thoughts. This is what caused me to renew my mind.

That transformation means we no longer have to conform to the patterns of this world. We can think differently, live differently, and respond differently.

Some of the ways I learned to replace my thoughts with God's thoughts were through journaling, confessing, meditating, and reading the Word of God.

My mentor taught me this very important exercise, which I mention from my book, *Memoirs of Singlehood and the Steps Toward Marriage*: Get a journal and write all your thoughts—good, bad, or ugly—for five minutes, then go back and read what you wrote. If you see any thought contrary to the Word of God, replace it with a scripture.

So, when thoughts would come to me and say, "God could never love a person like me," I would write the Scripture reference next to that thought: Nothing can separate me from the love of God (Romans 8:38).

This exercise helped me change the way I thought in many areas of my life. I quickly recognized what was happening in my mind and countered it with the Word.

There was a time when fear seemed so big in my life, and it was overtaking me. By journaling, I saw that I wasn't fearful in every area—it was fear about a situation at work or a confrontation I needed to make. The Holy Spirit gently showed me it was only one or two things, not that I was a fearful person.

Have you felt like you were angry, depressed, or fearful? Try this for a few days. You might realize that it's not everything; it's one or two areas that need your attention. This exercise may help you feel less overwhelmed and give you the courage to fight back.

Reading the Word builds your faith. Meditating on it causes an image of success to rise up within you. Joshua 1:8 says, "This

Book of the Law shall not depart from your mouth, but you shall meditate in it day and night... Then you will make your way prosperous, and then you will have good success."

YOUR INNER IMAGE MATTERS

Proverbs 23:7 says:

"As a man thinks in his heart, so is he."

You can only go as far as your inner image allows.

Renewing your mind is daily work.

But every day you choose God's thoughts — hope rises a little higher.

WHAT DOES GOD SAY ABOUT THOUGHTS?

- We have the mind of Christ (1 Corinthians 2:16)
- Meditate on the Word, day and night (Joshua 1:8)
- Take every thought captive (2 Corinthians 10:5)
- Be transformed by renewing your mind (Romans 12:2)
- Take no anxious thought (Matthew 6:31)

REFLECTION QUESTIONS

1. What are you thinking about most right now?
2. Are your thoughts moving you forward or pulling you backward?
3. How often are you feeding your mind with God's Word?
4. What thought patterns need to be uprooted?
5. What truth about yourself do you need to believe again?
6. Are you choosing life with your thoughts — or reacting from fear?
7. What does choosing life look like today?
8. What pain are you running from?
9. What life-giving thought will you begin repeating daily?

ACTION STEP

This week, read God's Word at least four times.

Choose one Scripture.

Write it.

Speak it.

Picture yourself living it.

Then ask: What would my life look like if I truly believed this?

CHANGE YOUR WORDS, CHANGE YOUR LIFE.

- Joyce Meyer

CHAPTER 5

WHAT ARE YOU SAYING?

THOUGHTS DON'T STAY SILENT FOR LONG. IF YOU DON'T stop the thought, it becomes words, and before long, those words start shaping your life.

YOUR WORDS CREATE YOUR WORLD

There are over one million words in the English language. Most people know around 20,000 words, speak around 150 words per minute, and use close to 16,000 words a day.

So yes, your words matter. But it's not about how many words you say each day, it's about which words you choose and why you choose them. If you look at your life and don't like what you see, it is time to examine what you've been saying.

God created the world with words.

Genesis 1:3 says: "And God said, 'Let there be light,' and there was light." God didn't think light into existence. He spoke it.

The same God who formed the world with His words says that we can do the same.

Hebrews 11:3 tells us, "By faith we understand that the worlds were framed by the word of God, so that what is seen was not made out of things which are visible." How was it made visible? By the words that were spoken.

In *Never Run at Your Giant with Your Mouth Shut*, Mark Hankins says,

> Hebrews 11:3 says that in the beginning God "framed" the worlds with His Words. Everything we can see was framed with an unseen substance called faith. Faith is always made up of the spoken word of God. Everything we can see was made out of words and the devil has gotten into people's lives and framed a false picture that is not in God's plan.

Recognize this: everything you keep saying, you will eventually keep seeing.

When you go into people's homes, you see pictures of loved ones on the walls, on tables, and even throughout your own home. Those pictures bring happiness. They remind you of the people you love, both those who are still here and those who have passed.

So imagine this.

> ***Since we speak thousands of words a day, we have thousands of chances to speak life.***

Everything in your life up until this point has been framed by your words.

How have you framed your world?

If someone walked into your house, what would those frames be filled with?

Would they show a new house, promotions, bonuses, marriage, a new baby?

Or would they show sickness, debt, lack, just enough, and broken relationships?

You choose what goes in the frames with your mouth.

SPEAK WHAT YOU WANT, NOT WHAT YOU SEE

Moving forward in faith starts with a choice.

As I mentioned earlier, each day you get to choose how it will go. In Deuteronomy 30:19, God tells us to choose life, not death; blessings, not curses. And then He gives us the answer to the open book test: "Choose life, so that you and your descendants may live."

One of the first things I say in the morning is: "Thank You, Jesus, for waking me up today." Or: "Good morning, Holy Spirit." I don't do that because I'm trying to be "super spiritual." I do it because I've learned that the tone of my day is often set by the first words out of my mouth. I'm acknowledging God, and I want His direction for my life, which is His Word.

By the time a person is 18 years old, they may have heard the word "no" 148,000 times.

And since we speak thousands of words a day, we have thousands of chances to speak life.

Before you open your mouth, remember:

Your words carry power—power to heal or harm, to build or break, to release hope or reinforce fear.

Jesus said in Matthew 12:37:

"For by your words you will be justified, and by your words you will be condemned."

DID YOU KNOW?

Dr. Shad Helmstetter, author of *What to Say When You Talk to Your Self*, wrote that by the time a person is 18 years old, they may have heard the word "no" 148,000 times.

That is a lot of negativity.

That is a lot of limitations.

That is a lot of words working against your confidence, your identity, and your future.

No wonder so many people struggle with what they say to themselves.

But today, it's time for yes.

Yes to life.

Yes to peace.

Yes to healing.

Yes to what God says about you.

You do not have to keep repeating the negative words that were spoken over you.

You can speak something different.

You can say what God says.

And when you consistently speak life, it will begin to change what you believe.

YOUR BODY IS LISTENING

I remember hearing a family member say for years, "This just gets on my nerves." One day, she developed a pinched nerve that caused excruciating pain. She remembered that God brought those very words back to her memory. She repented, changed her words to life-giving ones, and asked God for healing, and He delivered her.

I also heard a story about someone who constantly said, "This pisses me off." Over time, they developed serious kidney issues and had trouble urinating. It was as if their body had been following the instructions their mouth had been giving it for years. Their words weren't just expressions; they were declarations.

I'm not saying every health condition is caused by one sentence.

I am saying we often don't realize how much we speak over ourselves until life starts repeating what we've been rehearsing.

COMMON THOUGHT PATTERNS THAT SHAPE YOUR LIFE

Have you ever noticed how certain phrases roll off your tongue without thinking? They may sound harmless... but repeated words become mental pathways. And mental pathways become habits.

Here are some examples of common thought patterns many people live by:

- "I can never remember people's names."
- "It always rains on my days off."
- "Every year I get sick with the same thing."
- "I never have enough."
- "My car always breaks down."
- "I'm not smart."
- "I'm not creative."
- "I'm always anxious."
- "I worry about my family constantly—I can't help it."
- "That makes me so mad."
- "I'm too old."
- "I'm too young."
- "I could never afford that."

- "I'll never make it."
- "What's the point of trying?"
- "I can't change."
- "I can't lose weight."
- "I have a slow metabolism."
- "It's too late."
- "Life's not fair."
- "I'm not talented enough."
- "I'm broke."
- "I'm a loser."
- "No one would ever want me."
- "I don't have what it takes."
- "I'll always be alone."
- "I'll never get married."
- "I can't pay for that."
- "I'll never have that."
- "I'm just clumsy."
- "This job is killing me."
- "I'm always so tired."
- "I can't catch a break."
- "Everything I eat goes straight to my thighs."
- "I always mess things up."
- "No one listens to me."
- "I'm terrible with money."
- "I get nervous every time I have to speak."
- "I could never start a business."
- "Nothing ever works out for me."
- "I'm cursed."

- "That's just my luck."
- "People always let me down."
- "Good things don't happen to people like me."

Proverbs 18:21 says:

"Death and life are in the power of the tongue."

That's a warning and an invitation.

At first, they sound like "just talking."

But over time, they start sounding like the truth. And that's how strongholds form, not overnight, but over repetition.

THREE WORDS OF LIFE

Research in positive psychology has shown that positive interactions are important for our emotional well-being. Psychologist Barbara Fredrickson proposed the 3:1 positivity ratio.

Her research suggests that people tend to flourish when they experience about three positive interactions for every one negative one.

Why does this matter?

> ***Our minds remember criticism longer than encouragement.***

Because negative words tend to carry more weight. Our minds remember criticism longer than encouragement. One discouraging comment can linger in someone's heart far longer than we realize.

That's why it often takes several positive words to counter the impact of just one negative one.

That shows just how powerful our words really are.

So, if it takes three positive words to outweigh just one negative one, imagine the difference we could make if we intentionally chose to speak life-giving words more often.

After all, Scripture reminds us:

"Kind words are like honey—sweet to the soul and healthy for the body." (Proverbs 16:24 NLT)

STORIES THAT STICK

Let me show you what I mean with some examples below:

"I'm always sick around the holidays."

A family friend used to say every year, "You know I always get sick around the holidays. It's like clockwork." She would even prepare for it—stocking up on medicine as Thanksgiving approached. And just like she said, every year—flu, cold, sinus infection—something would show up. One year, after hearing a message about speaking life, she decided to change her words. Instead of predicting sickness, she said, "This year I'm healthy, joyful, and full of peace." That year was the first time she stayed well, and the pattern never returned.

"I'm losing my mind."

A man in his early 60s would constantly say, "I'm losing my mind," any time he forgot something or misplaced his keys. It became a joke—he'd say it in front of his family, laugh it off, and keep going. Years later, when he started showing early signs of dementia, his daughter remembered those words. "He's been saying that for decades," she said. "He spoke it over himself like it was harmless." She now teaches her children to say the opposite: "I have the mind of Christ. My memory is sharp and clear.

"I don't belong here."

A young woman always said, "I don't fit in anywhere," or "I just don't belong." It started in school and followed her into adulthood. Those words took root—she struggled with loneliness, job insecurity, and even with friendships. One day during a coaching session, she realized she had never believed she was welcome anywhere. She had spoken rejection over herself before anyone else could. Once she started replacing those words with truth, "I belong. I am accepted. I bring value." Her confidence changed, and doors began to open in places she once felt invisible.

"I'm just big-boned."

This one came from an aunt who always said, "Our family is just big-boned—we don't lose weight." It was her answer to every health challenge, every doctor's visit, and every opportunity to try something new. But over time, that belief turned into hopelessness. She stopped trying altogether because she already "knew" she couldn't change. Years later, after watching someone else in the family transform, she became curious—and stopped saying that phrase. Instead, she began saying, "I can make healthy choices. My body responds well to change." And wouldn't you know, her body started doing just that.

Words don't just describe your life. They direct it.

FROM NEGATIVE TO POSITIVE: WORD REPLACEMENT LIST

If you want to see a change in your life, you have to change your language. Start speaking God's language, His Word.

Start here:

Negative Phrase	Positive Replacement (Speak Life)
I never have enough.	God supplies all my needs according to His riches. (Phil 4:19)
I'm always anxious.	I have the peace of God that passes all understanding. (Phil 4:7)
I'm too old.	I am fruitful in every season. (Ps 92:14)
I can't change.	I am being transformed by the renewing of my mind. (Rom 12:2)
I'm broke.	I am blessed and highly favored. (Deut 28:6)
I'll never get married.	God is writing my story, and His timing is perfect. (Hab 2:3)
I'm always tired.	The joy of the Lord is my strength. (Neh 8:10)
I'm not smart.	I have the mind of Christ. (1 Cor 2:16)
I'm a loser.	I am more than a conqueror through Christ. (Romans 8:37)
Nothing ever works for my out for me.	God is working all things together good. (Romans 8:28)
I'll always be alone.	God sets the lonely in families. (Psalm 68:6)
I can't lose weight.	My body is a temple of the Holy Spirit; I honor it. (1 Corinthians 6:19-20)

Don't just read these. Say them. Hope rises when your mouth starts agreeing with God again.

THE RICE STORY: THE PROOF IS IN YOUR WORDS

I once heard a fascinating story about Dr. Masaru Emoto, a Japanese researcher and alternative healer whose experiments sparked widespread conversation about the power of words and intention. He became well known when his water molecule experiments were featured in the 2004 film *What the Bleep Do We Know?* His research showed that human thoughts and words could alter physical reality—specifically, the molecular structure of water.

Given that the human body is composed of at least 60% water, his observations raise important questions. Can we really afford to speak carelessly or carry negative thoughts?

One of his famous demonstrations was his rice experiment. He placed portions of cooked rice into two separate containers. On one, he wrote "thank you," and on the other, "you fool." He had schoolchildren say those labels out loud each day. After 30 days, the rice labeled "thank you" looked almost unchanged, while the one labeled "you fool" was moldy and rotten.

I'll be honest, I wanted to know if this experiment would really work, so I tried it for myself. I needed proof—not only to build my faith but also to be more mindful of the words I spoke over my own life.

I used three mason jars filled with cooked rice. I labeled one jar "love," another "ignore," and the third "hate." I placed them on my kitchen counter where I would see them daily.

- For the "love" jar, I spoke kind, affirming words: "I love you," "You're amazing."
- For the "ignore" jar, I acted like it didn't exist, by waving my arm and turning my head as if to reject it.
- For the "hate" jar, though it was uncomfortable, I spoke negative words just for the sake of the experiment.

After 30 days, the results were shocking:

- The "love" jar had almost no mold and even smelled sweet.
- The "ignore" jar was half-covered in mold.
- The "hate" jar? Thick, black mold covered it almost completely.

I was amazed! I could tangibly see the effect of my words by how the rice responded. If rice, a lifeless grain, can respond to words, how much more do our minds, bodies, and spirits respond to what we declare every day?

Are there areas in your life that feel "moldy" or decayed places where you've unknowingly spoken defeat over yourself? Or are there areas of peace and growth, the "sweet-smelling" places, where you've chosen to speak life?

Jesus said in Mark 11:23, "You will have whatever you say." Instead of talking about your mountain, start speaking to it. God's Word is your weapon.

TRY THIS (THE "AND THAT'S JUST THE WAY I WANT IT" CHECK)

Terri Savelle Foy, known as the "Cheerleader of Dreams," gives this simple advice: "Every time you speak, add this phrase: 'and that's just the way I want it.'"

"I never have enough money... and that's just the way I want it."

Your life today is the result of the words you spoke yesterday.

"I'm too old to change...and that's just the way I want it."

"I'll be single the rest of my life... and that's just the way I want it."

Those words will stop you in your tracks. If you don't want it, don't say it. Speak what you want, not what you see. Romans 4:17 says, "Call those things which be not as though they were."

Your life today is the result of the words you spoke yesterday, but the good news is—you can change your future starting right now.

When you begin to say what you want instead of only what you see, things begin to change. Romans 4:17 reminds us to call those things that are not as though they were. Your life is shaped by what you have believed—but you can begin changing it with your words.

WHAT SCRIPTURE IS THAT?

Here is a good rule of thumb: My mentor has said this to me for many years, and everyone who knows her knows this phrase:

"What Scripture is that?" I even made buttons with it once, and one time it was written on a cake for her. I was in her office one day many years ago, telling her about what was bothering me at the time. I'm sure whatever I was saying was full of doubt. She told me to look in my Bible and find what I was saying in there.

So, there I was, picking up my Bible and acting like I was looking through it to find it. She stopped me and said, "It's not in there."

I laugh now because I really thought I was going to find it in there. Then she said, "If it's not found in the Word of God, you have no business saying it out of your mouth."

So, the next time you want to speak about anything, make sure what comes out of your mouth is the Word of God. Remember, every word you speak is a prophecy over your future.

WATCH YOUR CIRCLE

Be mindful of who you allow into your space. I talk more about this in chapter seven, but I want to mention it here, because it is important. If you constantly hang around people who speak fear, worry, or doubt, it can slowly influence your own language and beliefs more than you realize.

If the people around you aren't speaking life, peace, encouragement, or faith, it's okay to love them from a distance. You can still be kind without giving their words permission to shape your future.

Dr. Robb Thompson, would say: "There are two types of people: those who bring you closer to God, and those who pull you away. Matthew 7:16 says, "You will know them by their fruit."

And Luke 6:45 reminds us, "Out of the abundance of the heart, the mouth speaks." In other words, what's in you will eventually come out, and the people around you will see it and hear it.

Be intentional. Choose your words wisely, and choose the people around you wisely, too.

REFLECTION QUESTIONS

1. Have you caught yourself speaking negative words over your life?
2. What are 3 phrases you say often that need to be replaced with truth?
3. What did you learn from the Rice Experiment?
4. Are there people in your life whose words affect your own speech?
5. What do you want your words to produce in the next season?

CHALLENGE

- Try the Rice Experiment for yourself.
- Share your results with me on social media.

EVERY DAY MAY NOT LOOK GOOD, BUT YOU CAN FIND GOOD IN EVERY DAY.

- Ericka Glorious Moore

CHAPTER 6

WHAT ARE YOU LOOKING AT?

WHAT YOU LOOK AT AND HOW YOU VIEW IT WILL determine which direction you will go. Focus is everything.

What you keep looking at affects how you feel, what you believe, and how you move through life. When you change the way you look at things, the things you look at will change.

If you keep rehearsing all your hurts, shortcomings, disappointments, and fears, you will get more of it. But if you begin to lift your eyes and look at what God has done, what He is doing, and what is still possible, things can begin to look different.

One of the ways you can change your life is by changing your perspective of what you see.

PERSPECTIVE SHAPES WHAT YOU SEE

Our perspective is like the pair of glasses we wear to look at the world. And a lot of the time, we do not even realize we are wearing them. The way we see life is often shaped by our experiences, our pain, our upbringing, our environment, and the beliefs we have formed along the way.

That means two people can walk through the same situation and walk away seeing it completely differently and having two different outcomes. Why? Because we are not just responding to what happened. We are responding through the filter of what we believe. And that matters more than most people realize. Because perception often becomes reality.

You live according to what you truly believe.

Not always because it is the full truth, but because it is the truth we have come to believe. That is why renewing your mind matters so much.

It is about allowing God to change the lens through which you see everything.

And one of the simplest ways to begin shifting your perspective is through gratitude.

GRATITUDE LIFTS YOUR EYES

I once heard someone say that the richest person on earth is a person of gratitude. I believe that is true. Because gratitude has a way of lifting your eyes. It helps you stop staring at what is wrong and start recognizing what is still right. It reminds you that even if everything is not perfect, that there is still something to be thankful for.

Google defines gratitude as the quality of being thankful; readiness to show appreciation for and to return kindness. It means we are grateful for what we have and show appreciation.

Gratitude is not just a nice idea. It is something God tells us to practice.

So how do we actually do that?

Here is a simple way to begin.

QUICK GRATITUDE CHECK (YES OR NO)

Sometimes it feels like you don't have anything to be grateful for, and it's easy to overlook the smallest things. But let's do a simple exercise together.

Stop and ask yourself these questions and answer honestly.

- Do I have food, shelter, and clothing?
- Do I have someone who cares about me? Family, friends, etc.
- Has God helped me before?
- Has He answered even one of my prayers?
- Has He ever shown me favor in a situation I didn't expect?
- Has He ever provided for me financially, even in a small way?

If you answered "yes" to even one...then you already have more to be grateful for than you may realize.

And no, that does not mean everything in your life is easy.

It just means you are choosing not to let situations and circumstances dictate how you will look at life and choose to be grateful.

> ***In many ways, gratitude is connected to faith.***

In many ways, gratitude is connected to faith.

It is choosing to trust God and believe He is still working, even when everything around you may not look like it.

4 A'S OF GRATITUDE

While gratitude is a wonderful practice and a gift, here is how we can foster a grateful mindset God's way by using the four A's of Gratitude.

I came across a simple practice in an article called *5 Benefits Gratitude Has on the Brain*, and it really helped me see gratitude in a deeper way.

1. Appreciation

This is simply recognizing what God has already done.

When you begin to notice His blessings, provisions, big or small. You start to see how present He really is in your daily life. (Psalms 103:2)

2. Approval

Gratitude grows when we stop living for people's approval and start living for God's.

There is a different kind of peace that comes when you know you are walking in step with Him. You're no longer trying to please everyone else. You're simply focused on being who God has called you to be.

3. Admiration

Sometimes we focus so much on what we need that we forget to reflect on who God is.

When you take time to admire His character, His love, and His faithfulness, your heart begins to fill with gratitude. Before we ask God for anything, we need to first thank Him for all He has already done.

It keeps your mind on what is good. And if He helped you before, He will do it again. (Philippians 4:6–7)

4. Attention

Gratitude requires focus.

You have to be intentional about where your mind goes. When

you shift your attention back to God and His promises, it begins to quiet the noise. What once felt overwhelming starts to feel more manageable.

1 Thessalonians 5:18 says to give thanks in all circumstances, for this is God's will for you in Christ Jesus.

That means we can still find something to thank Him for, even in the middle of difficult situations, not just the good ones.

That is a different way of living.

And it takes intention.

THE BENEFITS OF GRATITUDE

Research shows that gratitude can have a real impact on your mental and emotional well-being.

In a well-known 2005 study connected to the University of Pennsylvania, researchers found that practicing gratitude was linked to greater happiness and lower levels of depression. In other words, gratitude can help shift your focus away from what is wrong and remind you of what is still good.

When your mind feels overwhelmed, negative thoughts can begin to sound louder than the truth. But gratitude helps interrupt that pattern. It gives your mind something life-giving to return to.

Some of the benefits of gratitude include:

- More peace in your mind
- A healthier outlook
- Better emotional health
- Stronger relationships
- Greater resilience during hard times

When you slow down long enough to recognize what is still good, gratitude becomes a way of life. It gives your heart and mind something healthy to hold onto. It also helps you focus on all the victories you have experienced up to this point in life. If God did it before, He will do it again. And that hope is often what helps you keep going.

GRATITUDE OR COMPLAINING

Gratitude and complaining lead you in two very different directions. No matter where you are in life you have something to be thankful for. And when you express gratitude, your life will begin to improve. Your health, your finances, your opportunities, your relationships. Life attracts life.

Steve Harvey once said that gratitude is a powerful process. The only way to move to the next level is to show gratitude for where you are. When you are grateful, it helps move you forward quicker. But the opposite is also true. Complaining can keep you stuck longer than you were ever meant to stay.

We see this clearly in the story of the Israelites. What should have been a two-week journey ended up taking forty years. Why? Because of complaining, doubt, and unbelief.

> ***The only way to move to the next level is to show gratitude for where you are.***

They saw miracles. They were delivered. God provided for them. And yet, they kept focusing on what they did not have instead of what God had already done.

Because of that, those who were twenty years old and older did not enter the Promised Land. That really made me think. It shows us that how we think and what we say can affect where we go.

Joyce Meyer says it like this: "You complain, you remain."

And if we are honest, we can see this pattern in our own lives.

Do you ever find yourself dealing with the same conditions year after year?

Barely making it.

Getting sick at the same time each year.

Not getting the promotion.

Still struggling to lose the weight.

Living with a poverty mindset.

It is connected to what you are consistently thinking and saying.

This is what many people refer to as the law of attraction. What you continually focus on and speak, you begin to see show up in your life, whether it is good or bad.

And think about this.

Do you enjoy being around someone who constantly complains?

I know I don't.

But when you are around someone who is grateful, something happens. When you bless them and they are thankful, kind, and appreciative, it makes you want to give more.

Gratitude attracts more.

Complaining repels it.

I used to be one of the complainers. The "woe is me" person. I would speak the Word in one moment, and then speak complaints in the next. And my prayers were being canceled out. When you complain and worry, you don't believe there is a solution to your problem. It is also selfish and not trusting God.

But now, I choose to be a person of gratitude in all things.

So when something is not going the way I think it should, I thank God for helping me through. I ask for His wisdom.

Because I know this:

If I thank Him in advance, everything will work out. Maybe not the way I think it will, but it will work out for my good.

I am kept in peace.

I bear much fruit.

I grow in faith.

And God gets all the glory for how He brings me through.

Gratitude is choosing to acknowledge that even in the middle of difficulty, there is still something good to see.

Remember, there is always something to thank God for.

Sometimes gratitude sounds like this:

- Thank You, God, that I'm still here.
- Thank You, God, for my family.
- Thank You, God, for loving me.
- Thank You, God, that You have a plan for me.

That kind of gratitude changes you. It softens your heart, shifts your thinking, and reminds you that God has been moving, even when you did not fully see it.

And once you begin to see differently, you begin to live differently, too.

MAKE GRATITUDE A DAILY PRACTICE

One thing that has helped me is keeping a gratitude journal. I have been doing this for years.

Every day, I write down at least three things I am grateful for.

Some days they are big things.

Some days they are small things.

But over time, it has trained me to notice God's goodness more.

You can do this too.

You can start with a gratitude journal, but you can also create a gratitude jar.

You can use something simple, like a mason jar. I kept mine on the counter in my kitchen so I would see it every day and be reminded to write down at least one thing I was grateful for.

Get some small pieces of paper, enough for 365 days of the year. I went to the dollar store and bought 3.5 x 5 colored index cards and cut them in half.

Every day, write down one thing you are grateful for and place it in the jar.

At the end of the year, you will have 365 reminders of God's goodness.

Just imagine being able to look back and see all the ways He kept you, provided for you, protected you, comforted you, and carried you.

That alone can change how you begin to see your life.

REFLECTION QUESTIONS

1. What are three things you can be grateful for today?
2. What have you been focusing on lately — pain, fear, lack, or God's faithfulness?
3. What is one hard area of your life where you need to ask God to help you see differently?
4. What has God already brought you through that you need to stop overlooking?
5. How can gratitude become a daily practice in your life?

PART II

THE INNER WORK

GOD IS MORE INTERESTED IN YOUR FUTURE AND YOUR RELATIONSHIPS THAN YOU ARE.

- Billy Graham

CHAPTER 7

WHO'S IN YOUR INNER CIRCLE?

YOU BECOME LIKE THE PEOPLE YOU CONSISTENTLY spend time with. And as you pursue peace, healing, and identity in Christ, one of the most important questions you can ask yourself is this: Who are you becoming because of the people around you?

Not just people you know. Not just people you're connected to.

I'm talking about the people who sit closest to your thoughts, your goals, and your spiritual core.

Because we often think about healing and peace in terms of what we do. But sometimes, it's not about doing more, it's about discerning more. Because while peace is personal, it's also relational.

The people around you are either helping you move forward or silently pulling you back. And when you're trying to heal, your circle matters—because what's around you can either help or hinder that process.

YOUR RELATIONSHIPS AFFECT YOU MORE THAN YOU THINK

Brian Tracy says that 85% of your success in life is determined by the people you spend the most time with. And when I look back over my own life, I can say this without hesitation:

Your inner circle shapes:

- Your thinking patterns
- Your beliefs about yourself
- Your emotional stability
- Your trust in God
- Your peace of mind

Sometimes the battle isn't just what you're facing—it's who you're facing it with.

Sometimes the battle isn't just what you're facing — it's who you're facing it with.

WHEN I HAD THE WRONG CIRCLE

This part is sometimes still hard to talk about because it takes me back to a time in my life when I didn't want to be here anymore. But I often wonder: Would it have gotten that dark if I had been in a safe environment and supportive relationships?

At the time, my friendships were filled with pressure to fit in, a lack of boundaries, fear of sharing my feelings, and, most importantly, I didn't feel safe. I wore masks and hid what I really felt inside. And when I finally broke down, the people around me didn't have the capacity to help.

One friend gave me an ultimatum—either choose her friendship or lose it. And this was during one of my lowest moments. I had to let her go. Another friend betrayed me by siding with someone at work who had mistreated me. That betrayal stung.

Then there was the friend I confided in, someone I told I was having suicidal thoughts and that I had a plan in mind. She brushed it off and said, "Oh, I've had those thoughts too," not realizing I was reaching out for help in desperation.

On the day I nearly followed through with my plan, I was talking to a family member and was met with, "I can't handle you being sad—because what would I do?"

Something broke in me. It deepened my hopelessness, and it was one of the reasons I ended up in the hospital.

Just days after being released, I saw missed calls from another friend who was upset because I didn't answer. She never asked where I was or why she hadn't heard from me in a couple of days. It was all about her and what she needed. That hurt even more.

The following weekend, I felt anxious because I knew I was stepping back into the same environment with the same people.

My mentor saw me and asked, "Who are these people you're surrounding yourself with?"

Then she said something that stayed with me:

"If you don't change who you hang around, you're going to end up right back in the hospital."

And that was my wake-up call.

HOW I MOVED FORWARD

Part of my healing came from taking inventory of the people around me.

I asked myself:

- Can I be my true self around them?
- Or am I constantly walking on eggshells?
- Am I always pouring out while no one is pouring into me?

Then I made a plan.

First, I left the stressful job that was draining my energy.

Then I evaluated my relationships and asked tough questions:

- Are they safe?
- Is this a win-win, or am I the one giving all the time?
- Can I be vulnerable without being judged or criticized?

I started choosing people more wisely.

I stopped chasing relationships that depleted me.

I began looking for mutuality and safety.

And it was hard at first—opening my heart again, trusting that I could be loved without having to earn it.

But little by little, I began to heal.

And as I did, new people came into my life.

I learned how to protect what God was restoring in me.

Psalm 101:6 (TPT) says: "My innermost circle will only be those whom I know are pure and godly. They will be the only ones I allow to minister to me."

Did you catch that? "The only ones I allow." That means you have a say. You can be intentional about who gets close.

LEVELS OF RELATIONSHIPS

Jennie Allen, best-selling author of Find Your People, teaches something powerful: not everyone deserves the same level of access. Here's her breakdown:

1. God – Always first.
2. Inner Circle – 2–5 people who know your soul deeply.
3. Village – Around 50 people in your community who support you.
4. Acquaintances – Everyone else.

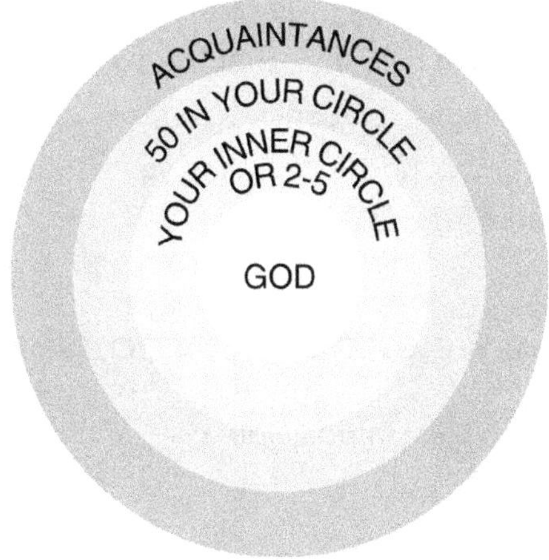

Illustration adapted from concepts in Jennie Allen, Find Your People

Jennie says your inner circle doesn't need to be big. It might include teachers, coworkers, church members, or your child's friends' parents. What matters most is:

- Availability – They show up.
- Courage – They'll say the hard things to help you grow.
- Humility – They can receive correction and give it with love.
- Transparency – You can be real with them.
- Accountability – They help you follow through.
- Consistency – They're present regularly, even when it's inconvenient.

And don't forget this: You can't have what you're not willing to become. Want trustworthy, honest friends? Be one. Want grace-filled friendships? Extend grace.

You can't have what you're not willing to become.

This takes action. Go get coffee. Stop by each other's houses. Watch a movie. Open up your life to them. This is especially vital if you're single.

As a single woman (thanking God in advance for my husband!), I know how easy it is to go home, shut the door, and stay isolated. But fulfilling, meaningful relationships require vulnerability. You have to be seen, heard, and known. And you might just be the answer to someone's prayer.

THE WEIGHT OF RELATIONSHIPS

Your circle doesn't just impact your day—it affects your direction.

Ask yourself:

- Who do you run to when you're uncertain?
- Who has access to your vulnerable thoughts?
- Who protects your peace—or provokes your panic?

Scripture speaks directly to this:

1 Corinthians 15:33 – "Do not be misled: 'Bad company corrupts good character.'"

Proverbs 13:20 – "Walk with the wise and become wise, for a companion of fools suffers harm."

Let's look at some examples below of good and bad relationships.

BIBLICAL EXAMPLES OF INNER CIRCLES

- Samson and Delilah: Samson let someone into the most sensitive part of his life who did not honor his calling—and it cost him everything.
- Jesus and the Disciples: Out of all His followers, Jesus had 12 close ones, and among those, Peter, James, and John were

His inner circle. He didn't isolate—but He was selective.

- David and Jonathan: A powerful example of covenant friendship. Jonathan protected David and even stepped back from the throne because he saw God's hand on David's life.
- Rehoboam: He rejected the wisdom of elders for the flattery of friends, and it tore the nation apart.
- Job's Friends: Sometimes, the wrong words from the right people can still create emotional damage.

IT'S NOT JUST WHAT YOU'RE FACING—IT'S WHO YOU'RE FACING IT WITH

Sometimes your anxiety isn't coming from the problem itself; it's coming from the people you're walking through it with. Sometimes your exhaustion isn't from the battle, it's from the constant background noise of the wrong voices around you.

You weren't created to isolate, but to choose. God cares about who surrounds you.

Even Jesus had Judas in His circle. But Jesus understood purpose and boundaries. Sometimes, the betrayal reveals the boundary, and that boundary protects your peace.

HABITS ARE CONTAGIOUS

Let's talk facts. This isn't just an opinion; research supports it. What's around you shapes what grows in you. Your circle doesn't just influence your mood; it shapes your habits, mindset, behavior, success, and even your mental and spiritual well-being. Who you hang around matters deeply, and the data proves it.

A study from the New England Journal of Medicine found that:

- If your friend becomes obese, your risk of becoming obese increases by 57%.
- If a friend quits smoking, you're more likely to quit too.
- Healthy habits like regular exercise and balanced eating? Those are contagious, too.

The people closest to you can quietly pull you toward peace or toward chaos.

So, what does that mean for you?

The people closest to you can quietly pull you toward peace or toward chaos. Over time, you begin to normalize whatever they normalize. That's why your mindset, emotional health, and even your physical habits often mirror those of your closest relationships.

MENTAL HEALTH MIRRORS THE ROOM

When you're surrounded by uplifting, faith-filled, goal-driven people, you feel more supported, more hopeful, and more equipped to face life's challenges. But when you're around people who drain you, criticize you, or live in constant fear, your spirit begins to reflect that environment.

Your mental health isn't just shaped by therapy or prayer—it's also shaped by your circle.

SUCCESS IS SOCIAL

Research from the Harvard Business Review suggests that about 85% of job success comes not from technical skills, but from soft skills like:

- Communication
- Teamwork

- Relationship-building

Translation? The quality of your relationships can directly impact your career growth, promotion potential, and professional confidence.

That coworker who celebrates your wins? That mentor who challenges you to grow? They're not just "nice to have"—they're strategic for your future.

ENVIRONMENT DRIVES BEHAVIOR

A Stanford study showed that your environment, especially your relationships, triggers or reduces temptation, helps or hinders discipline, and either feeds your faith or your fear.

The more you surround yourself with peace-filled people, the more peace you'll walk in.

The more you surround yourself with intentional, focused individuals, the more disciplined you become.

YOU ARE WHO YOU HANG AROUND

Here's the simple truth: people are watching you. And whether you realize it or not, who you hang with shapes what they assume about you—and what you begin to believe about yourself.

If you consistently associate with people who gossip, complain, and settle, eventually, you'll begin to reflect that mindset.

But, if you're surrounded by visionaries, truth-tellers, and people of prayer, you'll rise. Not because you're copying them—but because you're becoming more of who God called you to be.

Here's what I've learned:

- If you're around people with no goals or dreams, eventually you'll start to lose yours.

- If you're around people who are driven, spiritually anchored, and stretching toward purpose—you will be too.
- And if you're not currently surrounded by people, you admire or aspire to be like—go find them. They exist.

God is a relational God—and He created you for connection.

Whether it's online, in a mastermind group, at a church event, or even in your DMs, pursue community on purpose. It's okay to outgrow circles that no longer reflect your values. It's okay to create space for new people that match your healed mindset.

Your future self will thank you.

God is a relational God—and He created you for connection. You weren't meant to live alone, cry alone, celebrate alone, or make decisions alone.

Your peace is worth protecting. Your relationships are worth evaluating. Your future is worth being intentional about. Choose wisely.

REFLECTION QUESTIONS: INNER CIRCLE INVENTORY

Take a moment to reflect. Be honest, be prayerful, and be willing to reposition if needed.

1. Who are the top five people you spend the most time with?
   - Write their names down. Then ask yourself:
     - → Do they reflect my values, faith, and future goals?
2. Do these relationships help fuel my purpose—or drain my peace?
3. Who do I turn to when I feel overwhelmed, discouraged, or uncertain?
   - Do they point me back to God? Or add to my confusion?

4. Do I feel safe, seen, and supported in these relationships?
   o Can I share my struggles without being judged or dismissed?
5. Who inspires me right now—spiritually, emotionally, professionally?
6. Who speaks life over me consistently? Who challenges me to grow?
7. Which relationships require me to shrink, perform, or hide who I really am?
8. Is there someone in my life that I may need to lovingly reposition or create boundaries with?
9. Do I have friends who pray with me? Speak truth in love? Call me higher?
10. Am I the kind of friend I'm praying for?
    o If not, what fruit do I need to start cultivating?
11. Is God nudging me to step into a new community, group, or circle?
    o What's one step I can take this week to obey that nudge?
12. If Jesus were choosing my inner circle, who would He invite—and who might He lovingly distance?

WELLNESS CORNER: ACTION STEP

This week, do one thing on purpose:

- Identify one relationship that strengthens your peace—reach out and deepen it.
- Identify one relationship that drains your peace—pray, set a boundary, and reposition with love.

Small shifts create big futures.

PRAYER

God, thank You for caring about every part of my healing—not only what I think, but who I'm connected to. Give me discernment. Give me courage. Help me choose relationships that honor the future You're building in me. Heal what people mishandled. Restore what betrayal tried to steal. And plant me in a safe community—where hope can grow strong. In Jesus' name, amen.

NO ONE CAN MAKE YOU FEEL INFERIOR WITHOUT YOUR CONSENT.

- Eleanor Roosevelt

CHAPTER 8

DOES IT REALLY MATTER? (Q-TIP)

ON THE ROAD TO MENTAL HEALTH AND FREEDOM, you begin developing a stronger inner foundation, not hard or guarded, but grounded. When your affirmation, identity, and trust come from God, you stop searching for validation everywhere else.

THE Q-TIP PRINCIPLE

One of the greatest skills you can develop is emotional strength and learning to root your identity so deeply in God that you stop looking for affirmation everywhere else.

I want you to remember this every time you see a Q-TIP: Quit Taking It Personally.

Think of it like this: Q-Tips clear out what doesn't belong. And that's exactly what this principle does for your heart and mind. It clears out offense, assumptions, and unnecessary hurt so you can hear God's voice louder than the noise of other people's opinions.

Because when you stop taking things personally, you stop carrying battles that were never yours to fight in the first place.

SECURE IN WHO YOU ARE

I think about a woman I know, one of the kindest, gentlest

people I've ever met. She reminds me of Mary Poppins, grace-filled, calm, almost floating when she walks into a room.

What always amazed me was this:

Her husband rarely gave compliments, and it didn't bother her.

She once said, "I don't need compliments. I'm already loved by God."

That stayed with me.

Because that kind of security isn't natural, it's cultivated.

And honestly... it became something I wanted for myself.

WHEN SENSITIVITY TAKES OVER

Have you ever been called "too sensitive"? I have. For years, I took everything to heart until I realized that much of what I was reacting to had little to do with me. That sensitivity often stemmed from unresolved rejection. And that's why the Q-TIP principle is such a game changer.

I first heard this years ago from Dr. Robb Thompson, who said, "All problems are personal and internal."

What people say or do often reflects what's going on in their lives, not yours.

When we stop making everything about us, we give ourselves the gift of freedom. We stop living under the weight of imagined offenses. Because the truth is, most people are not thinking about us nearly as much as we assume.

Winston Churchill once said,

"When you're 20, you care what everyone thinks; when you're 40, you stop caring what everyone thinks; when you're 60, you realize no one was ever thinking about you in the first place."

There is deep freedom in that realization. This is the inner work.

CHOOSING GOD'S VOICE OVER EVERYONE ELSE'S

There was a time when I constantly sought advice from everyone, my pastors, friends, older sister, dad, mom, and anyone willing to listen. I doubted my own ability to make decisions because of past mistakes. If you had anything to criticize or critique about me, I would take it personally right away.

All problems are personal and internal. - Dr. Robb Thompson

I cried a lot; almost every time you saw me, I was upset about something. It could have been something I did right, but it was mostly what I did wrong or thought I did wrong. I automatically took the blame in all situations because I just wanted to be accepted.

Can you relate? Have you ever felt that way?

But one day, I decided I was going to just believe what God said about any situation and trust His guidance, knowing He wouldn't lead me into anything that would harm me.

One of my favorite scriptures that I have personalized and say almost every day is Proverbs 3:5-6: Lord, I trust you with all my heart. I lean not on my own understanding; in all my ways, I acknowledge you, and you will direct my steps. I also trust God throughout the day by asking for His help.

I remembered doing this for years, and one day, I looked up, and I wasn't crying all the time. I also realized that I wasn't running to everyone for help for every little thing. I started running to God first and did what I believed He told me to do. I was much more peaceful and confident in God and my own choices.

I remember telling my pastor that I noticed a change in my life. She said, "Now you have saved the church seventy-five dollars." I asked, "What do you mean? She said, 'Because you don't need to use all the tissue from all the crying." We laughed.

I'm grateful I can laugh now, because in the past, I never thought I'd get there

Hope strengthens when you stop handing your emotions to every passing opinion.

HOW WE TAKE THINGS PERSONALLY

Sometimes it looks like this:

- You get a new haircut, and no one mentions it – you don't feel pretty.
- A friend hasn't returned your text—you feel rejected.
- Your social media post got only a few likes—you feel overlooked.
- You hear about a party you were not invited to, and you don't feel like you fit in.
- You speak up during a meeting at work, but no one agrees with your suggestion, so you feel like your voice doesn't matter.

What do all these situations have in common? You assigned meaning to someone else's behavior without asking questions or offering grace.

WHAT'S REALLY HAPPENING?

Often, the narrative we create is a mix of assumptions and self-doubt. Our brain fills in the blanks with stories that align with past pain. So instead of being present and peaceful, we spiral into worry, offense, or false conclusions. We're hurt, but the truth is: we're the ones hurting ourselves.

Jesus is the ultimate example of not taking things personally. Even while being wrongfully persecuted, He looked at those who mocked, accused, and crucified Him and said, 'Father, forgive them, for they know not what they do.' And then He willingly gave His life for our sins.

If Jesus could respond with that kind of love and forgiveness, surely, with His help, we can, too.

FEAR VS LOVE

Here is something I learned:

God said fear believes the worst and love believes the best. It's your choice.

Ask yourself: If this person truly loves me, would they intentionally try to hurt me? And if I really believed the worst about them, would I even want this relationship?

When we operate in fear, we assume rejection. When we operate in love, we extend grace.

MY FEAR OF AUTHORITY

For a long time, I was afraid of authority figures, at work, at church, even at home. Whenever someone in authority wanted to meet with me, my mind immediately jumped to the worst-case scenario.

Have you ever done that? A boss asks to meet, a leader calls your name, a friend says they need to talk, and suddenly your thoughts spiral. Fear starts writing a story before the conversation even happens.

That was me. I assumed the worst before I even knew the truth. Looking back, I realize much of that reaction was rooted in fear and insecurity. It shaped many of my relationships until I learned to believe the best about myself and about others.

When we choose kindness and grace, we stop interpreting every situation through fear. Instead, we begin to pause and ask, what if this isn't bad? What if there's another perspective?

Philippians 4:7-8 encourages us to meditate on what is true, honorable, and good. In other words, train your mind to consider the best case scenario instead of the worst.

When we love our neighbors as ourselves, we begin to extend grace rather than assume, and that changes how we experience every conversation.

WHEN YOU FEEL OFFENDED - PAUSE

So, the next time you feel hurt, ask yourself these questions:

- Will this matter in 24 hours? In a week? In a year?
- Did I hear the full story?
- Could they be going through something themselves?
- Is this about me, or is this just triggering an old wound?

Give yourself space to reflect. Don't respond in the moment. Create distance so your reaction isn't automatic—it's prayerful.

CHOOSING GRACE OVER REACTION

- Choose curiosity over assumptions. Ask, "What else might be true?"
- Start giving people the benefit of the doubt.
- Anchor your identity in Scripture. (Galatians 1:10, Colossians 3:12–14)

- Ask God to help you see people through grace, not wounds.

REFLECTION QUESTIONS

1. What is one recent situation where you realized you may have taken something too personally?
2. How can you use the Q-TIP reminder to protect your peace this week?
3. What scriptures or affirmations help you stay grounded when you feel offended?
4. Who in your life do you need to extend grace to instead of taking their actions personally?
5. How would your life change if you no longer gave offense the power to steal your joy?

JOURNAL PROMPT

"Lord, help me see what offense I've been carrying. What moments did I take personally that weren't really about me? Teach me how to walk in freedom and let go." Write it down, forgive yourself and others, and let it go.

Q-TIP REMINDER

Keep one in your purse or tape one to your mirror. Remember: You don't have to carry everything.

When you stop taking everything personally, your heart will have peace to grow.

WHEN YOU GET LOTS OF REJECTIONS, YOU STOP FEARING IT. THIS MAKES YOU UNSTOPPABLE.

- Dr. Kaushik Sridhar

CHAPTER 9

COURAGE OVER REJECTION

ONCE YOU STOP TAKING EVERYTHING PERSONALLY, something powerful begins to happen. You start moving differently.

You stop shrinking to avoid discomfort. You stop waiting for perfect conditions. And eventually you realize there's one more step toward freedom:

Learning to ask, even when rejection feels possible.

Because let's be honest: inaction never taught me anything. Rejection? That taught me how to grow.

It showed me what I was made of. For a long time, I believed staying in my comfort zone was "safe." But here's the truth: comfort zones are illusions. What you're calling safety is actually silent suffering. You're not protecting yourself—you're pausing your potential.

FEAR OF REJECTION HELD ME BACK FROM EVERYTHING I WANTED

Have you ever stopped to ask yourself, "What has fear of rejection cost me?"

For me, it was:

- A fulfilling career
- Deep, nourishing friendships
- A relationship with someone special
- Peace of mind
- And the joy that comes from fully showing up in life

I thought I was "playing it safe" by not trying, by avoiding confrontation, by never asking for what I truly wanted. But that was a lie. I was stuck. Years passed. And one day I looked up and realized, I hadn't moved forward at all.

Same job. Same salary. Same car. Same emotional rut. Same unfulfilled dreams.

THE BAMBOO GROWTH STORY: REJECTION IS ROOT WORK

Bamboo is one of the fastest-growing plants in the world. In fact, some species have been recorded growing up to 35 inches in a single day. But that kind of growth does not happen without support underneath the surface. Bamboo spreads through an underground system called rhizomes, which helps sustain the growth you eventually see above ground.

Rejection can feel the same way.

Every "no" can make it seem like nothing is happening.

You pray, you try, you knock on doors—and it feels like the doors are not opening.

But what you don't see is what God may be building underneath the surface:

Roots.

Resilience.

Character.

Faith.

Strength.

So don't quit just because you can't see it yet. Because what God is building in you now may be the very thing that holds up what He does through you.

And when your season comes? You won't just grow a little; you'll experience a breakthrough that looks sudden and feels like overnight success. But it's not overnight. It's the result of years of hidden preparation.

But you will know it was built in the hidden places.

Don't quit in the middle of the process.

So, don't stop in the middle of the process. Keep watering the dream. Keep showing up. Because the "yes" you've been waiting for might be only one more ask away.

PROVERBS AND WISDOM IN ACTION

Proverbs 27:12 (MSG) says: "A prudent person sees trouble coming and ducks; a simpleton walks in blindly and is clobbered."

To be prudent means to be wise, discerning, and intentional. I knew if I wanted to live the life God had placed in my heart, I had to choose wisdom. Fear of people's opinions wasn't wisdom, it was bondage.

WHAT HELPED ME SHIFT: THE POWER OF REJECTION

During that season, I came across a powerful book called

Rejection Proof by Jia Jiang. His story challenged me in the best way.

Jia was living what many would call the "American Dream": a six-figure job, a happy marriage, a beautiful home. But inside, he felt unfulfilled. His real dream was to become an entrepreneur. After a failed pitch to an investor, he was paralyzed by rejection until he decided to do something wild.

He launched a 100-day Rejection Challenge, intentionally asking for outrageous things just to get rejected.

Some of his asks included:

- Asking a security guard for $100
- Requesting a donut shaped like the Olympic rings
- Asking to play soccer in a stranger's backyard

And to his surprise, some people actually said yes—and in the process, he learned that rejection isn't personal. Sometimes, the answer is no for reasons that have nothing to do with you.

MY OWN (UNOFFICIAL) 100-DAY REJECTION CHALLENGE

Inspired by Jia, I made a list of things I'd been too afraid to ask for. And then...I started asking.

- I reached out to Mignon Francois. Her story of turning $5 into a multimillion-dollar cupcake empire moved me deeply. I messaged her on Instagram and—within 21 minutes—she replied. Four days later, she called me personally and poured into me for thirty minutes. I cried at my desk. The very person I was afraid to ask made time for me.
- I messaged Dr. Michelle McKinney Hammond. Her books helped shape my life. I asked her for a Zoom call. She didn't have time—but she invited me to send questions instead. I did, and she responded to every single one.

- I asked a friend for help getting to a Notre Dame game. During my breast cancer journey, the story of Rudy Ruttiger from Notre Dame—the inspiration for the movie Rudy—became deeply personal to me. It represented hope and fight. A friend offered to help—and his dad bought me a $260 ticket so I could sit with their family. That "ask" turned into a memory I'll never forget.

Fear of rejection is a common emotional struggle that many people face.

I have also learned how to handle the word "no". I don't take it personally. I trust God and ask for another way. My way was not correct, so I let God lead.

It has been an eye-opening journey. What I have realized so far is this: far more people are willing to help you, give you the answer, and really care about you more than you realize. I am just getting started and will never return to the girl who never found out whether it was a yes or a no.

UNDERSTANDING REJECTION

Fear of rejection is a common emotional struggle that many people face. Rejection can feel deeply personal, but it often has more to do with timing, circumstances, or another person's limitations than your worth.

Research shows that social rejection can activate some of the same areas of the brain associated with physical pain. That helps explain why rejection can feel so intense and why many people avoid situations where they might hear "no."

Mental health experts also note that fear of rejection often keeps people from asking for help, applying for opportunities, speaking up, building relationships, or pursuing goals they truly desire.

These truths remind us that fear of rejection is common—but it is also conquerable. Rejection may sting for a moment, but it does not define your value, your future, or what God can still do in your life.

5 WAYS TO BUILD COURAGE OVER REJECTION

1. When You Don't Ask, the Answer is Already No

"You miss 100% of the shots you don't take." — Wayne Gretzky

Imagine walking past a door every day, wondering what's behind it—but never turning the knob. That's what not asking feels like. When you're afraid to speak up, pitch your idea, or share your dream, you silence your own potential.

Give yourself permission to ask. Ask for help. Ask for the meeting. Ask for the discount. Ask to be on the panel. Ask for what you're worth.

2. Fear Makes Cowards Out of Dreamers

"Feel the fear and do it anyway." — Susan Jeffers

Fear often disguises itself as logic. It tells us, "Now is not the right time," or "You need more credentials," or "You're not ready yet." But the truth is, we let fear lead far too often—and it causes dreamers to stay stuck.

When I was afraid to launch, I justified it with planning. When I was scared to be seen, I hid behind perfectionism. Sound familiar? Fear will always knock—but you don't have to answer the door.

3. Give Yourself Permission to Be Seen

Hiding doesn't protect you—it paralyzes you. I had to learn that playing small wasn't humility—it was fear in disguise. The world doesn't benefit from your hiding. You were created to be a light. And light doesn't ask for permission to shine, it just shines. So, show up. With flaws. With fears. With faith.

4. The Growth Is in the Go

Growth doesn't happen in your head. You can vision board, plan, and rehearse all you want—but transformation lives in movement. I remember my first design contract—I asked for $15,000. I didn't think they would accept the offer; instead, they said, "Where do I sign?"

5. No's Don't Kill - Silence Does

Every successful person has a pile of "no's" behind them—but they're not remembered for those. They're remembered for their yeses.

The 'no' might sting, but it doesn't stop you. The only thing that truly stalls your progress is doing nothing. So, pitch the book. Start the business. DM the guest you want on your podcast. Put yourself in position.

The right yes is waiting, but it needs to find you moving.

Remember this: if it can't harm you, don't let it scare you.

REFLECTION QUESTIONS

1. What dream or opportunity have you talked yourself out of because you feared rejection?
2. Which is worse: hearing "no" today or living with the regret of never asking?
3. Who are the people you've been scared to reach out to—and what's really stopping you?

4. When was the last time you felt truly proud of yourself for taking a risk?
5. If fear wasn't a factor, what's one thing you'd do today?

FINAL THOUGHTS

If you've felt stuck, afraid, or paralyzed by rejection, you are not alone. But staying in fear won't take you where your heart knows you're meant to be.

Here's what I want you to know. Rejection isn't the enemy. Inaction is. You won't die from a "no," but you might miss your purpose if you don't ask. And most of all, God's got your back.

BOUNDARIES ARE,
IN SIMPLE TERMS,
THE RECOGNITION OF
PERSONAL SPACE.

- ASA Don Brown

CHAPTER 10

BOUNDARIES: FREEDOM IN EVERY "NO" & POWER IN EVERY "YES"

IF I COULD GO BACK AND TEACH MY YOUNGER SELF anything, it would be this: Learn boundaries early.

It would have saved me heartache, stress, wasted time, and honestly, a lot of tears.

But guess what? It's never too late to course-correct. I'm living proof that when you finally learn how to honor yourself with boundaries, your entire life begins to change, from your relationships to your inner peace.

I first discovered this lesson by diving deep into the book Boundaries by Dr. Henry Cloud and Dr. John Townsend. I didn't just listen to it once —I listened to it on repeat until it soaked into my spirit and I finally got it.

What blew my mind was realizing how everything—your money, your friendships, your health, your emotions, your career, and even your dreams—is connected to your ability to set clear, healthy and loving boundaries.

Boundaries aren't optional.

They are essential to your growth, and your ability to thrive.

WHEN BOUNDARIES ARE MISSING, PAIN STEPS IN

Before we explore the solution, let's look at a few real-life scenarios. As you read them, notice if any feel familiar—because this is how missing boundaries quietly show up in everyday life.

Example #1: The "Go-To Person"

Imagine a young professional, eager to make a good impression at work. Every time a coworker needs help, they say yes—even if it means staying late, skipping meals, and taking work home on the weekends. At first, it feels good to be the "go-to person." But slowly, the weight of constant yeses turns into exhaustion, resentment, and burnout. One day, their body says, "Enough." They end up physically sick, emotionally drained, and wondering if they even like their job anymore.

Helpful Fact: According to the American Institute of Stress, about 80% of workers feel stress on the job, and nearly half say they need help learning how to manage it.

80% of workers feel stress on the job, and nearly half say they need help learning how to manage it.

Boundaries aren't just for relationships—they are survival tools.

Example #2 The "Fixer"

Picture someone who's always the "fixer" in their friend group. Whenever someone has a crisis—relationship drama, money problems, emotional breakdowns, they're the first call.

At first, it feels good to be needed. But over time, they start feeling drained. Their own needs go unnoticed. Their dreams get delayed because they're too busy carrying everyone else's burdens.

Eventually, they realize: Being a good friend doesn't mean being everyone's emergency room.

Helpful Fact: Research from the Mayo Clinic shows that healthy friendships improve your health and happiness, but unhealthy, one-sided relationships increase anxiety, depression, and burnout.

Boundaries allow you to show up for others without losing yourself.

Silent Sufferers: Are You One of Them?

You might be a silent sufferer if:

- You hate conflict.
- You always put others first, even when it hurts.
- You say yes with your mouth but scream no in your heart.

If this sounds familiar, good news: You're not broken—you're just overdue for stronger boundaries.

SO, WHAT EXACTLY IS A BOUNDARY?

A boundary is simply this: A line that defines what is okay and what is not okay. I like to think of boundaries as fences with gates. You decide who gets in, who stays out, and how much access they have to you. Without gates, without clear boundaries, anything and anyone can trample your peace.

Here are four areas where boundaries matter most:

1. Money: Learning to say no to financial guilt trips.
2. Physical Space: Choosing who touches you, hugs you, or even stands close to you.
3. Relationships: Deciding the level of access people have to your heart and time.
4. Emotions: Taking responsibility for your own feelings—and not for everyone else's.

FREEDOM FROM DEPENDENCY

Growing up, I leaned heavily on my dad and sister for decisions, emotional support, and even spiritual direction. That dependency didn't disappear; it morphed into friendships, jobs, and even ministry opportunities. It wasn't until I learned to lean on God first that I stood tall on my own two feet.

Helpful Fact: People who maintain strong, healthy boundaries report higher self-esteem, better mental health, and greater life satisfaction (American Psychological Association).

LEARNING TO SAY NO WITHOUT GUILT

When I spoke at a school event, I asked students what life skills they wished they had learned earlier. One of the top answers: "I wish I knew how to say no." Saying no doesn't make you mean. It makes you honest and healthy. You are allowed to disappoint people—and still be a loving, good person.

When I started setting boundaries in my relationships, I didn't just notice a change, I felt it.

Peace came back. Joy started to feel possible again.

And I realized something: It wasn't about cutting people off. It was about finally choosing what was healthy for me.

HOW TO PUT BOUNDARIES INTO PRACTICE: THE 4 COLUMN RULE™

For years, I found myself trapped in win-lose patterns—pouring out my time, energy, and heart at work, with friends, and even with family, until I was completely drained. Then everything changed. I discovered a simple but powerful tool I call The 4 Column Rule.

This helped me move from guilt-driven decisions to wisdom-driven decisions, from constant depletion to healthy, win-win relationships. And now I want to show you how to use it.

The heart of the 4 Column Rule principle comes from 2 Corinthians 9:7: "Every man, as he purposes in his heart, so let him give; not grudgingly, or of necessity, for God loves a cheerful giver."

In other words, we're called to give from peace—not guilt, fear, or obligation.

Here's how to put it into practice:

Step 1: Draw Your Four Columns

Grab a blank sheet of paper (or open a fresh note on your phone) and divide it into four vertical columns.

Label them:

1. Willingly
2. Cheerfully
3. Necessity
4. Grudgingly

Step 2: Map Your Commitments

Under each heading, list every major activity, relationship, or obligation you have:

- Willingly — Things you look forward to and embrace with open arms.
- Cheerfully — Tasks you handle gladly, even if they require effort.
- Necessity — Responsibilities you must do, but that don't light you up.
- Grudgingly — Actions you resent or feel forced into.

Step 3: Evaluate Before You Say Yes

The next time someone asks for your time, money, or energy, pause and ask yourself:

- Am I doing this willingly?
- Am I doing this cheerfully?
- Or is this out of necessity or grudgingly?

If your honest answer lands in Necessity or Grudgingly, give yourself permission to step back, pray or reflect, and reconsider the request.

Helpful Tip: Take 5 minutes—or sleep on it—before you commit.

Step 4: Rebalance Your Columns Regularly

- Weekly Check-In: Review your lists at the end of each week. Are new items creeping into "Necessity" or "Grudgingly"
- Practice Small No's: Start by declining low-stakes requests to strengthen your boundary muscles.
- Pray or Reflect: Ask God (or reflect internally) for the wisdom to see clearly which commitments align with your purpose.
- Choose from Joy: Whether you say "yes" or "no," let your decision come from a place of peace, not guilt.

WHY THIS WORKS

Clarity: You see exactly where your energy goes.

Empowerment: You learn to guard your peace by design.

Joy: You rediscover what lights you up—and release what drains you.

4 COLUMN RULE™

WILLINGLY	CHEERFULLY	NECESSITY	GRUDGINGLY

ericka
glorious moore

Check out the 4 Column Rule™ YouTube video here

Download the 4 Column Rule PDF: www.erickagloriousmoore.com/resources

Remember: Every time you say no to the things that weigh you down, you're saying yes to what truly matters.

And now that you've learned how to build healthy boundaries with the 4 Column Rule, the next step is learning how to walk in forgiveness, because boundaries protect your peace, but forgiveness protects your heart.

TRAINING PEOPLE HOW TO TREAT YOU

While building my business while working full-time, I had zero boundaries. Clients could call, text, or email me at any time, including weekends.

If a client said they needed me urgently, even if I was already on my way to work, I would turn around, go back home, and use my paid time off just to meet their needs. For years, I didn't take a single vacation day for myself because I spent them all on clients.

Needless to say, this way of living was not sustainable. I was exhausted, burned out, and quietly resentful. That's when I decided something had to change.

I created a couple of clear boundaries:

1. Office Hours: I told my clients they could only reach me during specific times of the day. If they contacted me outside of those hours, I didn't reply until the next business day. Was it hard? Absolutely. I didn't want to disappoint anyone—but I knew I had to protect my health and peace.
2. Rush Fees (or at least the threat of them): I stopped doing last-minute, super-fast turnarounds for free. I told clients that if they needed something immediately, it would come with a rush fee. Funny enough, once I mentioned the fee, most of them suddenly discovered it "wasn't that urgent after all."
3. At first, some clients didn't like it. A few kept calling at all hours, texting late at night, and even acting frustrated when I didn't respond immediately. But I stayed consistent. I didn't argue, I didn't over-explain—I simply stuck to my boundary.

And you know what happened? They eventually adjusted. Once they saw I was firm, they respected my new rules. In fact, many started planning ahead because I trained them to treat me differently.

Boundaries may feel uncomfortable at first, but once you enforce them consistently, you don't just change your habits; you retrain how others treat you.

REFLECTION QUESTIONS

1. Where do you most need to set boundaries right now?
2. What relationships or commitments drain you instead of energizing you?
3. How often do you say "yes" when you really want to say "no"?
4. What would your life look like if you only said yes to what brings you peace and joy?
5. How can you use the Four Column Rule this week to protect your mental health?

IF WE REALLY
WANT TO LOVE,
WE MUST LEARN
HOW TO FORGIVE.

- Mother Teresa

CHAPTER 11

100 WAYS TO FORGIVE AND LOVE

BOUNDARIES TEACH YOU WHERE YOU END AND someone else begins. They teach you what is yours to carry, and what is not. But here's what I've learned: Even after you draw the line, life still tests it. People still cross it. Words still land wrong. Old wounds still get touched. And when that happens, you have a choice.

You can build a life with strong boundaries and still carry a heavy heart. Or you can do the deeper work that makes your peace sustainable: forgiveness.

This chapter is an invitation into one of the most transformative acts for mental, emotional, and spiritual wellness, not because it excuses what happened, but because it releases you from having to live in it.

WHY FORGIVENESS MATTERS

Forgiveness is more than a spiritual instruction; it's a healing choice. In the Bible, God emphasizes forgiveness so deeply that He says, "Don't even bring your gifts to Me if you have unforgiveness in your heart. Make it right with your brother or sister first." (See Matthew 5:23–24)

As believers, we are ambassadors of love. If we walk around

harboring resentment, we aren't loving God, ourselves, or others. Forgiveness sets us free to love fully and live lightly.

WHEN FAMILIARITY BREEDS CONTEMPT

There's something powerful and painful about seeing someone up close. The more familiar we become with people, the more we notice their flaws. Yet it's in that vulnerability where the greatest kind of love can exist, the kind that mirrors Christ.

Because Jesus sees all of us: the good, the bad, and the ugly and loves us still.

I experienced this firsthand with my sister Tonya.

We lived together for seven years. At first, we were thrilled to have our own space. But over time, the everyday annoyances crept in: makeup on the clean hand towels, untidy shared spaces, little habits that rubbed me the wrong way.

Even the things I once loved about her began to frustrate me. I prayed to God to help me to appreciate her and not become familiar, and God gave me a clear instruction: "Write down 100 things you're grateful for about your sister."

At first, it felt impossible. I started with, "She is my sister." (I know—super basic!) But then, something miraculous happened.

Almost thirty items in, I began to cry. I wrote:

- "She told me about Jesus."
- "She taught me about the Holy Spirit."
- "She bought me my first Bible."
- "She's my biggest cheerleader."

Tears streamed down my face as my heart began to soften. I saw her again, not as flawed, but as my sister who loved me and had always been there for me.

All the good began to outweigh the bad, and I realized it wasn't really about her. It was about my expectations, my way of doing things.

Jesus said, "Why do you look at the speck in your brother's eye and pay no attention to the plank in your own?" (Matthew 7:3). When we're busy tending to our own growth, we won't have time to scrutinize others.

After I completed the list, the Lord prompted me to read it aloud to my sister. We sat down in the front room, and as I began, both of us started to cry. I apologized for becoming too familiar and focused on her flaws and became grateful to have her as my sister.

Dr. Robb Thompson, says, "Familiarity breeds contempt." We have to fight to keep our hearts open and see the people in our lives with fresh eyes, believing the best in them and loving them where they are, not where we want them to be.

LOVE LIKE JESUS

1 Corinthians 13:4–8 reminds us:

Love is patient. Love is kind. It keeps no record of wrongs.

Love believes the best. It covers faults. It never fails.

When we hold grudges, we open a door for the enemy to torment us with resentment, fear, and emotional bondage. The kingdom of God operates on love and faith, and you can't walk in faith with an empty love tank.

God calls us to love because we have the capacity to love. Even when it's hard. Even when we're hurt.

FORGIVENESS IS A WEAPON

Forgiveness doesn't say what happened was okay. It says: "I refuse to be chained to it any longer."

Someone once said, "Unforgiveness is like drinking poison and expecting the other person to die."

Unforgiveness traps you in the time it happened. You can see it in people who recount a past hurt and relive every detail, the date, the words, the clothes. It's as if no time has passed.

But God tells us to forget what lies behind and press forward. (Philippians 3:13–14)

JESUS FORGAVE, SO CAN WE

On the cross, Jesus said: "Father, forgive them, for they know not what they do" (Luke 23:34).

Then He gave up His life.

If He could forgive in that moment, surely, we can release the hurt we've carried.

Joyce Meyer says we should make allowances for each other's faults.

Try saying this like:

- "It's okay."
- "I make mistakes too."
- "I forgive you."
- "Don't give it another thought."

None of us are perfect, and every one of us will need grace at some point. Sow the kind of mercy, patience, and understanding you hope to receive when it is your turn to need it.

FORGIVENESS: FAITH OVER FEELINGS

Forgiveness is an act of faith, not a feeling. Think of it like a hot iron. Even after you unplug it, it stays hot for a while. But eventually, it cools. In the same way, you may choose to forgive someone, but your emotions might still feel raw for a time. That doesn't mean your forgiveness wasn't real. It just means your feelings haven't caught up with your faith yet.

Forgiveness is an act of faith, not a feeling.

Sometimes, after you've truly forgiven someone, you might see them, hear their name, or recall the hurt, and feel that familiar sting rise again. That's when you gently remind your heart: "I gave this to God. My feelings will catch up with my faith."

That's why God says, "Don't let the sun go down on your anger" (Ephesians 4:26). He knows that holding onto offense keeps us in bondage.

Forgiveness is His invitation to peace.

And yes, there are deeper wounds: abuse, abandonment, trauma. Those may require counseling, support, and time. And that's okay. Healing is a process. But the goal is always a healed heart. God doesn't want us living in torment. He wants us to live in freedom.

WHEN YOU STILL NEED TO HAVE THE CONVERSATION

Now, what happens when you've forgiven in your heart, but you still feel led to talk with the person who hurt you?

First, ask yourself:

- Why do I want to bring this up?
- Is it for closure, clarity, or reconciliation?

- What if they don't say what I hoped?
- What if there's no apology?

Or maybe it's something ongoing—something they're still doing; unaware it's hurting you or crossing a boundary. If that's the case, pause and pray. Ask God to guide your words and posture your heart in love before approaching them.

I once received some powerful advice about confrontation:

Believe the best.

Go in assuming they didn't mean to cause harm. Start with a gentle question like:

"When you said ________________, what did you mean by that?"

Let them answer. Then you can say:

"I don't think you meant to hurt me, but it did hurt."

This kind of honesty leaves room for grace and growth, not guilt and shame.

As Mike Murdock wisely says, "Pursuit is the proof of love." I've come to believe that confrontation can be a doorway to deeper intimacy. It's not about conflict, it's about care. You don't confront people you don't care about. You do it because the relationship is worth saving.

JOSEPH: WHAT YOU MEANT FOR EVIL

Joseph was betrayed by his brothers, thrown into a pit, sold into slavery, and wrongfully imprisoned. And when he saw them again, the Bible says he wept loudly behind closed doors. And then he invited them to dinner. He forgave them. He embraced them. He saw the bigger picture:

"What you meant for evil, God meant for good" (Genesis 50:20).

Forgiveness is not optional for believers. Jesus Himself said, "If you do not forgive others their sins, your Father will not forgive your sins" (Matthew 6:15).

We need His forgiveness daily, so how could we withhold it from others? This is why forgiveness is not just for them. It's for you. It unlocks your peace and restores your heart.

FORGIVENESS HEALS MORE THAN YOUR HEART

Forgiveness may feel hard, but it is deeply healing:

- Reduces anxiety and depression: Holding grudges increases stress levels and symptoms of anxiety and depression.
- Improves heart health: Chronic anger can lead to heart disease. Forgiveness lowers blood pressure and improves cardiovascular health.
- Boosts self-esteem: Forgiveness helps us see ourselves and others with compassion.
- Releases trauma responses: Forgiving helps the brain to rewire itself and shift from "threat" to "safety" mode.

A PRAYER FOR FORGIVENESS

Now, let's take a moment to pray. This is where you release it all to God:

Speak this aloud:

God, I release all grudges and pain in my heart. I forgive like Jesus forgives. Lord, I give You the hurt and pain of ______________.
I lift them up to You and let it go, never to pick it up again. If the pain resurfaces, I remind myself: I've already forgiven. I won't be deceived into rehashing what's been healed.
I receive Your peace. I choose to walk in love. I believe the best about myself and others. And I rest in Your grace.

WALKING IN LOVE

Now that you've prayed and released forgiveness, it's time to fill that space with love. Forgiveness clears the ground, but love plants the seeds for new life.

Declare this out loud:

1 Corinthians 13:4–8 (Personalized):

Love is patient with me, and I will be patient with others. Love is kind, I will choose kindness even when it's hard. Love does not envy or boast, it doesn't compete. Love is not proud, it walks humbly and with grace. Love does not dishonor others, it lifts them up. Love is not self-seeking, it serves. Love is not easily angered, it breathes and lets go. Love keeps no record of wrongs, today, I erase the list. Love always protects, always trusts, always hopes, always perseveres. Love never fails, and I choose to walk in that kind of love.

And here's what I love about this moment: Forgiveness doesn't just free you from what happened. It frees you for what's next.

THE I UNDERSTAND MOVEMENT

What began in September 2018 with one simple i understand Mental Health Awareness Cards grew into a message of hope, healing, and connection. Friends, family, coworkers, and members of the community shared words of encouragement that reminded others they were seen, valued, and not alone.

Sometimes the words people need most are simply:

I understand.

The card that started it all in September 2018. The front features the words *i understand*, and the back includes the National Suicide Prevention Lifeline and Crisis Text Line. It also provides space to write an encouraging message for someone in need of hope.

If you're thinking about suicide, are worried about a friend or loved one, or would like emotional support, the Lifeline network is available 24/7, confidential and free, across the United States.

National Suicide Prevention Lifeline: 1-800-273-8255 **Crisis Text Line:** 741741

If this card has helped and encouraged you, please share at www.facebook.com/IUnderstandGlobal

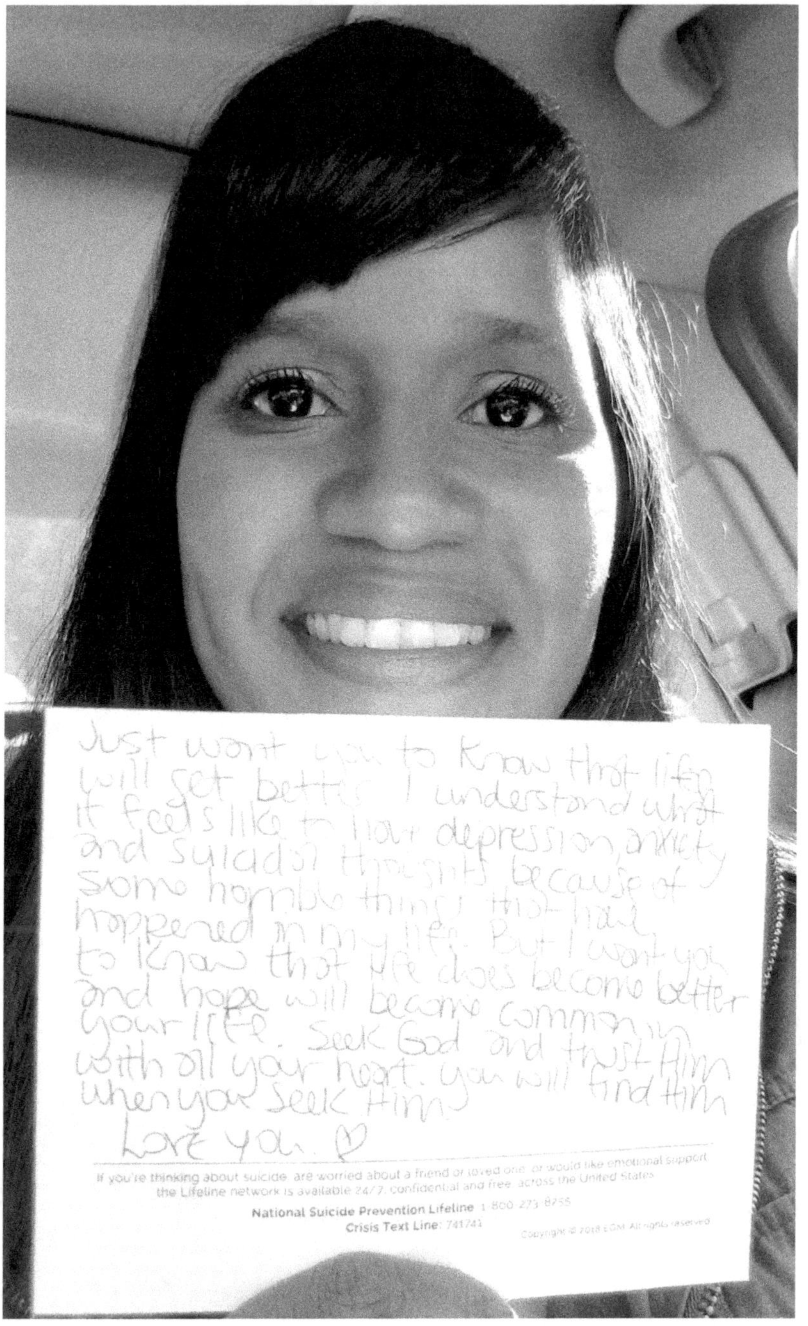

A simple message placed on my heart to help others feel seen and understood.

If you're thinking about suicide, are worried about a friend or loved one, or would like emotional support, the Lifeline network is available 24/7, confidential and free, across the United States.

National Suicide Prevention Lifeline: 1-800-273-8255 **Crisis Text Line:** 741741

If this card has helped and encouraged you, please share at www.facebook.com/IUnderstandGlobal

If you're thinking about suicide, are worried about a friend or loved one, or would like emotional support, the Lifeline network is available 24/7, confidential and free, across the United States.

National Suicide Prevention Lifeline: 1-800-273-8255 **Crisis Text Line:** 741741

If this card has helped and encouraged you, please share at www.facebook.com/IUnderstandGlobal

Copyright © 2020 EGM. All rights reserved.

If you're thinking about suicide, are worried about a friend or loved one, or would like emotional support, the Lifeline network is available 24/7, confidential and free, across the United States.

National Suicide Prevention Lifeline: 1-800-273-8255 **Crisis Text Line:** 741741

If this card has helped and encouraged you, please share at www.facebook.com/IUnderstandGlobal

Each day focus on one positive thing to be thankful
for, when a negative thought
enters your mind. always over-
Coming a neg thought with a
positive one. Ex. When you feel
unloved - Say God Loves me.

If you're thinking about suicide, are worried about a friend or loved one, or would like emotional support, the Lifeline network is available 24/7, confidential and free, across the United States.

National Suicide Prevention Lifeline: 1-800-273-8255 **Crisis Text Line:** 741741

If this card has helped and encouraged you, please share at www.facebook.com/IUnderstandGlobal

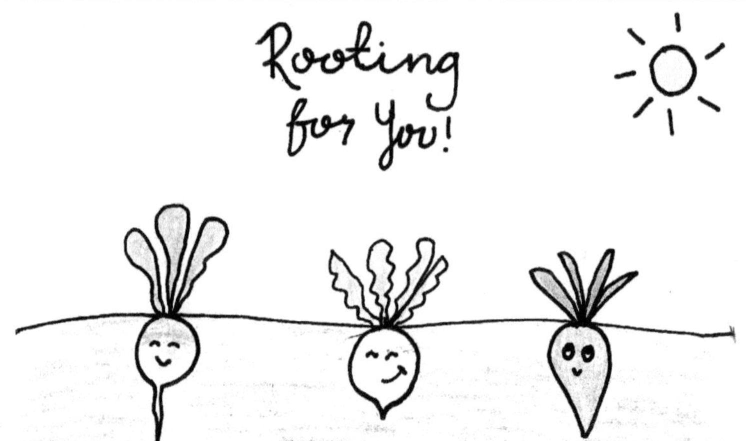

If you're thinking about suicide, are worried about a friend or loved one, or would like emotional support, the Lifeline network is available 24/7, confidential and free, across the United States.

National Suicide Prevention Lifeline: 1-800-273-8255 | **Crisis Text Line:** 741741

If this card has helped and encouraged you, please share at www.facebook.com/iunderstandglobal

God is concerned about everything that is going on in your life.

Psalm 138:8

If you're thinking about suicide, are worried about a friend or loved one, or would like emotional support, the Lifeline network is available 24/7, confidential and free, across the United States.

National Suicide Prevention Lifeline: 1-800-273-8255 **Crisis Text Line:** 741741

If this card has helped and encouraged you, please share at www.facebook.com/IUnderstandGlobal

If you're thinking about suicide, are worried about a friend or loved one, or would like emotional support, the Lifeline network is available 24/7, confidential and free, across the United States.

National Suicide Prevention Lifeline: 1-800-273-8255 | **Crisis Text Line:** 741741

If this card has helped and encouraged you, please share at www.facebook.com/iunderstandglobal

If you're thinking about suicide, are worried about a friend or loved one, or would like emotional support, the Lifeline network is available 24/7, confidential and free, across the United States.

National Suicide Prevention Lifeline: 1-800-273-8255 | **Crisis Text Line:** 741741

If this card has helped and encouraged you, please share at www.facebook.com/iunderstandglobal

If you're thinking about suicide, are worried about a friend or loved one, or would like emotional support, the Lifeline network is available 24/7, confidential and free, across the United States.

National Suicide Prevention Lifeline: 1-800-273-8255 | **Crisis Text Line:** 741741

If this card has helped and encouraged you, please share at www.facebook.com/iunderstandglobal

When life gives you lemons, use them to make cupcakes with lemon icing

If you're thinking about suicide, are worried about a friend or loved one, or would like emotional support, the Lifeline network is available 24/7, confidential and free, across the United States.

National Suicide Prevention Lifeline: 1-800-273-8255 | **Crisis Text Line:** 741741

If this card has helped and encouraged you, please share at www.facebook.com/iunderstandglobal

If you're thinking about suicide, are worried about a friend or loved one, or would like emotional support, the Lifeline network is available 24/7, confidential and free, across the United States.

National Suicide Prevention Lifeline: 1-800-273-8255 | **Crisis Text Line:** 741741

If this card has helped and encouraged you, please share at www.facebook.com/iunderstandglobal

If you're thinking about suicide, are worried about a friend or loved one, or would like emotional support, the Lifeline network is available 24/7, confidential and free, across the United States.

National Suicide Prevention Lifeline: 1-800-273-8255 **Crisis Text Line:** 741741

If this card has helped and encouraged you, please share at www.facebook.com/IUnderstandGlobal

If you're thinking about suicide, are worried about a friend or loved one, or would like emotional support, the Lifeline network is available 24/7, confidential and free, across the United States.

National Suicide Prevention Lifeline: 1-800-273-8255 **Crisis Text Line:** 741741

If this card has helped and encouraged you, please share at www.facebook.com/IUnderstandGlobal

If you're thinking about suicide, are worried about a friend or loved one, or would like emotional support, the Lifeline network is available 24/7, confidential and free, across the United States.

National Suicide Prevention Lifeline: 1-800-273-8255 **Crisis Text Line:** 741741

If this card has helped and encouraged you, please share at www.facebook.com/IUnderstandGlobal

If you're thinking about suicide, are worried about a friend or loved one, or would like emotional support, the Lifeline network is available 24/7, confidential and free, across the United States.

National Suicide Prevention Lifeline: 1-800-273-8255 **Crisis Text Line**: 741741

If this card has helped and encouraged you, please share at www.facebook.com/IUnderstandGlobal

If you're thinking about suicide, are worried about a friend or loved one, or would like emotional support, the Lifeline network is available 24/7, confidential and free, across the United States.

National Suicide Prevention Lifeline: 1-800-273-8255 **Crisis Text Line**: 741741

If this card has helped and encouraged you, please share at www.facebook.com/IUnderstandGlobal

PART III

WALKING IN WHOLENESS

SUCCESS IS
A SERIES OF
SMALL WINS.

– Jordan Peterson

CHAPTER 12

CELEBRATE THE WINS, CELEBRATE YOU

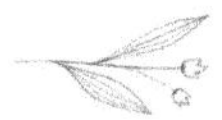

WHY CELEBRATING OUR WINS IS SO IMPORTANT. As an overcomer in Christ, I've learned the power of pausing to acknowledge progress. Whether it's getting out of bed on a hard day, choosing kindness when anger is easier, or finally finishing that task you've been putting off, those moments matter.

Celebrating your wins isn't just feel-good fluff. It is vital for your mental wellness and spiritual encouragement. Every time you celebrate a win, no matter how small, your brain gets a message: "I'm growing. I'm doing well. I'm moving forward." And that matters more than most people realize.

THE BENEFIT OF CELEBRATING SMALL WINS

Our brains are wired to respond to rewards.

That is why even small accomplishments matter more than we realize.

U.S. Navy Admiral William H. McRaven shared this powerfully in his commencement speech, "Make Your Bed," delivered to the graduates of The University of Texas at Austin on May 17, 2014.

He said that if you make your bed every morning, you will have accomplished the first task of the day. That one small act gives you a sense of pride and momentum. And often, one completed task leads to another... and another... and another.

By the end of the day, what started as one small win can turn into several.

That is the power of small wins.

They remind you that progress is happening.

And when you begin to recognize your progress, your confidence starts to grow.

WHAT HAPPENS IN THE BRAIN WHEN YOU CELEBRATE

Two powerful things happen in your brain when you start to celebrate your wins:

Dopamine Is Released – When you recognize progress, your brain's reward system activates. Dopamine is released, boosting your mood and increasing motivation. It's like your brain saying, "Let's do that again!"

You Train Your Brain to Look for the Good – Over time, celebrating wins helps rewire your thinking toward hope and possibility (positivity). As we learned earlier, that is called neuroplasticity. The Bible calls it renewing your mind (Romans 12:2). Every small win is proof that transformation is possible.

DON'T DESPISE SMALL BEGINNINGS

We live in a culture that celebrates the big moments, like the promotion, the graduation, and the business launch. But in God's Kingdom, the beginning matters.

God's Word says, "Do not despise these small beginnings, for the Lord rejoices to see the work begin." — Zechariah 4:10 (NLT)

Heaven rejoices not just when you finish, but when you start. When you pray for 5 minutes instead of scrolling, that's a seed. When you save $1 instead of spending it, that's a seed. When you drink a glass of water instead of a can of pop, that's a seed. When you forgive instead of holding onto anger, that's a seed.

It's easy to celebrate the big wins, but there can be long stretches in between them. That's why it's important to keep taking the next small step, because eventually, those steps add up.

Take Thomas Edison. It took him nearly 10,000 attempts to get it right. Most people would call that failure.

But he said, "I have not failed. I've just found 10,000 ways that won't work."

Heaven rejoices not just when you finish, but when you start.

He didn't focus on what wasn't working. He focused on what was moving him closer to his goal. And that's how we have to see it too.

The small steps you take today are building something bigger than you realize for tomorrow.

BE GRATEFUL IN YOUR PROGRESS

In Luke 17:11–19, Jesus healed ten lepers, but only one returned to give thanks. Jesus asked, "Were not all ten cleansed? Where are the other nine?" (v. 17)

There is something powerful about acknowledging what God has done. Gratitude unlocks more, and celebration keeps our hearts soft and humble.

David understood this. He celebrated victories often, and even in pain, he reminded himself of God's goodness. "Bless the Lord, O my soul, and forget not all His benefits." (Psalm 103:2)

Celebration doesn't ignore the hard. It highlights the hope. And helps you to keep going.

HOW ONE HABIT BUILT A LEGACY

Comedian Jerry Seinfeld built his legendary career using a simple system: write one joke a day. That's it. He didn't wait for inspiration; he committed to the habit. Over time, those single jokes stacked into miles of material.

He used what he called the "Don't Break the Chain" method: every day he wrote, he marked an X on the calendar. Eventually, the chain of X's grew so long that he didn't want to break it.

This is Zechariah 4:10 in action. Seinfeld didn't despise small beginnings—he kept showing up day after day.

One joke became hundreds, then thousands. That material turned into a show, and that show, Seinfeld, became one of the most successful television shows of all time. And over time, consistent small wins built a legacy.

THE POWER OF STACKING SMALL WINS

Here are more examples of how small wins add up:

- Read 1 page a day: In a year, that's 365 pages, an entire book.
- Save $1 a day: In three years, that's over $1,000 saved.
- Pray for 5 minutes a day: Over time, that habit deepens your relationship with God.
- Walk 10 minutes a day: In a year, that's more than 60 hours of movement.
- Write one affirmation daily: In 90 days, you've written 90 reasons to believe in yourself.

These are the wins that build discipline, confidence, and faith. They don't look like much in the beginning, but over time, they become the foundation for lasting transformation.

When you celebrate small wins, you teach your brain to keep going. You're not just building habits, you're building hope.

7-DAY SMALL WINS CHALLENGE (ACTION STEP)

For the next 7 days, track and celebrate your small wins:

1. Write down one small win each day.
2. Celebrate it out loud and thank God for it.
3. Share one win with a friend or accountability partner.
4. Reward yourself (big or small).
5. Repeat for 7 days and watch your confidence grow.

This isn't just a challenge; it's a mindset shift. By the end of the week, you'll have proof: you're not stuck. You're growing. And those small notes will become part of your story, one that builds confidence and faith.

REFLECTION QUESTIONS

1. How has God shown up for you in ways you might have overlooked?
2. What would it feel like to stack small wins instead of waiting for one big breakthrough?

AFFIRMATION

"I celebrate my progress, no matter how small. I am growing, healing, and becoming all God created me to be."

FAITH IS TAKING THE FIRST STEP EVEN WHEN YOU DON'T SEE THE WHOLE STAIRCASE.

- Martin Luther King Jr.

CHAPTER 13

GIVE YOURSELF PERMISSION

YOU ARE ALLOWED TO MOVE FORWARD. IT'S TIME to give yourself permission to have the audacity to have everything in all areas of your life.

Giving yourself permission to grow, dream again, and take chances may seem scary. But you need to open your eyes to what is possible. Choose to be courageous. Choose to believe God and go forward. If you are not moving forward, you will always drift back.

I GAVE MYSELF PERMISSION

Years ago, one night at 3 AM, I woke up and realized I was going through the same cycles in life. The same amount of money, the same job, the same people, the same weight, the same emotional bondage, the same relationships—everything felt the same.

But that night, I cried out to God, wanting something different. It became discouraging to see the same patterns year after year with no change. I wanted more.

I needed to be vulnerable again, to take chances, to open my heart to love and to be loved. Those were some of the things I desired.

So I opened my mouth, and the "I Give Myself Permission" affirmations were born.

I Give Myself Permission Affirmations

I give myself permission to:

1. Love myself and others (Mark 12:31)
2. Open my heart to be loved (Romans 8:38–39)
3. Forgive myself and my past mistakes (1 John 1:9)
4. Forgive hurtful words and actions by others (Ephesians 4:31–32)
5. Let go of past hurts and traumas (Philippians 3:13)
6. Be kind to myself and others (Ephesians 4:32)
7. Be patient with myself and others (1 Corinthians 13:4)
8. Conquer fear with love (1 John 4:18)
9. Let go of limiting beliefs (Philippians 4:13)
10. Live in the moment (Ecclesiastes 5:19)
11. Enjoy my life (John 10:10)
12. Be happy (Psalm 144:15)
13. Be successful (Joshua 1:8)
14. Take risks (Numbers 13:30)
15. Be hopeful (Hebrews 11:1)
16. Be my best self in every area of life (Romans 12:1)
17. Simply be me (Psalm 139:13–14)
18. Believe the best about others and myself (Luke 6:37)
19. Make wise decisions (James 1:5)
20. Have healthy boundaries (Matthew 5:37)
21. Build fulfilling relationships (Proverbs 27:9)
22. Dream big (Ephesians 3:20)
23. Accomplish big goals (Luke 1:37)
24. Be a trendsetter (Romans 12:2)
25. Trust God (Proverbs 3:5–6)

26. Be mentally, spiritually, emotionally, and physically free (John 8:36)
27. Respect myself and others (1 Peter 2:17)
28. Know I am worth it (Ephesians 1:5)
29. Be confident (Psalm 27:3)
30. Accomplish all the God-given dreams in my heart (John 17:4)

I laid back down in bed, and I felt a wave of calm and peace flood over me. I was able to go back to sleep, feeling encouraged.

When I woke up in the morning, I had hope in my heart and knew everything would be okay.

I realized they weren't just words. They were decisions.

And each decision I made with my mouth determined the direction I was going. I chose to release what was behind me and step into what was ahead.

Are you in an endless cycle of defeat, worry, and fear? Does your life feel like it's stuck on repeat?

Do you notice that you go through the same cycles, yet still desire change so desperately?

Is it time to give yourself permission?

Sometimes we think we are waiting on God to help us move forward, but really, God is waiting on us to make the first move (James 4:8).

Let's look at a moment when God was waiting on Moses.

WHEN GOD WAS WAITING ON MOSES

When the people of Israel stood in front of the Red Sea, everything looked impossible. The water was in front of them, the enemy was behind them, and they were waiting for something to happen.

This moment is found in Exodus 14, when the Israelites had just left Egypt and found themselves trapped with nowhere to go.

Before anything changed, Moses spoke to the people and said, "Do not be afraid. Stand firm, you will see the deliverance of the Lord" (Exodus 14:13).

Moses declared that they would be delivered before it happened, and God responded by telling them to move forward.

As it says in Exodus 14:15, "Why do you cry to Me? Tell the children of Israel to go forward."

Moses had already been given what he needed. He had the staff in his hand. He had the instruction. But nothing happened until he acted. He didn't stand there hoping the water would open. He followed the instruction he had already received.

Sometimes you are waiting on God, when God is waiting on you.

In Exodus 14:16, God told him to "Lift up your rod, and stretch out your hand over the sea and divide it."

Moses lifted his staff, and the waters opened.

This is a reminder that sometimes you are waiting on God, when God is waiting on you.

Waiting on you to act on what you already know.
Waiting on you to trust what He already said.
Waiting on you to use what you already have.

You may feel like nothing is changing, but the next step may not be waiting, it may be obedience.

Because just like Moses, you already have something in your hand. You already have what you need to succeed.

Motivational speaker Zig Ziglar said, "Many years ago as a young, aspiring speaker, I heard an older speaker who was quite philosophical say that you are where you because that's exactly where you want to be." Ziglar confessed, "I was broke, in debt and down in the dumps. It came through loud and clear that I was where I was and what I was because of the decisions and choices I had made in my life."

By giving yourself permission, you are finally taking responsibility for your life, your actions, and your decisions.

TAKE 100% RESPONSIBILITY

One of the false beliefs in our culture is that we are owed a great life—that somehow someone, somewhere is responsible for our happiness, success, opportunities, and relationships simply because we exist.

But the truth is, there is only one person responsible for the quality of your life—and that is you.

If you want to be successful, you have to take 100% responsibility for everything in your life, both good and bad. This includes your income, your fitness, your health, your relationships, your debt, your career, your thoughts, your emotions—everything.

> ***There is only one person responsible for the quality of your life—and that is you.***

This is not simple, but it is possible.

It's easy to blame others—your environment, your upbringing, your parents, your coworkers, your finances, or missed opportunities.

But the real issue still comes back to us.

I once heard a story about a man walking at night who saw another man on his knees searching under a streetlamp.

He asked what he was looking for.

"My key," the man replied.

So he helped him search.

After an hour, he asked, "Are you sure you lost it here?"

The man replied, "No, I lost it in my house, but there is more light out here."

It's time to stop looking outside yourself for answers to why your life has not changed.

Because you—and you alone—determine the direction and quality of your life.

Jim Rohn said, "You must take personal responsibility. You cannot change the circumstances, the seasons, or the wind, but you can change yourself."

So here are two ways to take one hundred percent responsibility.

1. Give up all excuses

You need to give up all victim stories, all the reasons why you can't succeed or why something feels out of reach up until now.

You need to draw a line in the sand and say, "I give it up for good."

All that matters from this point moving forward is that you choose to act as if you are 100% responsible for everything that does or does not happen to you.

2. Give up blaming

You will never become successful as long as you continue to blame someone or something for your lack of success.

If you want to be a winner, you have to acknowledge the truth. It is you who took the actions. No one can make you do anything.

Besides, all blame is a waste of time.

As Wayne Dyer said, "No matter how much fault you find with another, and regardless of how much you blame him, it will not change you."

You are the one who ate the hamburger and fries.

You are the one who chose not to say no.

You are the one who spent money you didn't have.

You are the one who chose your spouse.

You are the one who chose your job.

You are the one who chose your income.

You are the one who chose to compromise.

I am not trying to be harsh, but if we want the life of our dreams, we need to take an honest assessment of the thoughts we think, the feelings we create, and the choices we make. That is why we are where we are now.

THE DECISION IS YOURS

There is good news! We can give ourselves permission to make better choices—to choose God, to choose better habits, to choose better relationships, and to choose differently.

No one is coming to hand it to you, and no one is going to force you into it. You have to give it to yourself, just like I did.

That night at 3 AM, nothing around me had changed. My circumstances were the same, my situation looked the same, but I made a decision.

I gave myself permission to grow, to heal, to be vulnerable again, and to believe that my life could look different.

And that decision changed everything.

So now I want to ask you: what are you still waiting for permission to do? To forgive, to let go, to dream again, to take the step, or to become who God has already called you to be?

You don't have to wait anymore.

You can decide right now.

I give myself permission...

Finish that sentence.

Say it out loud.

Write it down.

Believe it.

Because your life begins to change the moment you do.

YOU WILL NEVER
LEAVE WHERE YOU ARE
UNTIL YOU SEE WHERE
YOU'D RATHER BE.

- Unknown

CHAPTER 14

WHERE ARE YOU GOING?

YOU'VE DONE THE WORK. YOU'VE FACED YOUR PAST. You showed up for your healing. You let go. You forgave. You said yes to peace. And you began believing in the value God placed on your life. But now what?

Now that the slate is clean, what picture are you going to paint? Because God didn't bring you this far just to bring you this far. You are the artist of your life.

VISION IS BIBLICAL

Throughout Scripture, God often gave people vision before He gave them victory.

Joseph had a dream at 17 that he would lead and rescue nations. It took years of slavery, prison, and injustice before that dream came true (Genesis 37).

Abraham was told to look at the stars because that's how numerous his descendants would be—even when he had no children. God gave him a vision of the impossible (Genesis 15).

Nehemiah had a vision to rebuild the wall of Jerusalem, and he used that vision to lead people into action despite opposition (Nehemiah 2).

David had to see himself killing Goliath before he ever released the stone (1 Samuel 17).

God often works through vision. He gives you a picture in your spirit before you ever see it in your hands. So let's talk about how to activate what He has shown you.

IMAGINE THE IMPOSSIBLE

Think of yourself, imagine yourself, and see yourself living your dreams in your mind. Everything gets started in your imagination first. You have to hold on to the thoughts that agree with your dreams because you become what you think about.

Your real life begins first in your imagination, not only in what you currently see in the natural. We have two different types of sight: natural sight and spiritual sight. Natural sight sees what is all around you. Spiritual sight sees within, sees the invisible, and sees what others cannot see.

Your real life begins first in your imagination.

Albert Einstein said, "Imagination is everything. It is the preview of life's coming attractions." Isaiah 43:19 says God is doing a new thing. Do you see it? Sometimes God is asking us what we see.

The simplest way to begin is to identify your desires. What keeps coming to your heart? What do you keep imagining? Pay attention.

DREAM BIG AND GET CLEAR

Now it's time to dream big. Identify what you want. Get clear on where you want to go. Write down what excites you. What are you passionate about? What do you love doing? If money were not an issue, what would you be doing as a career? Don't try to figure out how it's going to happen, just write it all down. Don't treat it like homework, this is the fun part.

If you're a football fan, you probably know Hall of Fame football coach, Lou Holtz, did this same exercise back in 1966. He was twenty-eight years old, out of work assistant football coach, when he lost his job, had a wife who was eight months pregnant, two children to support. His wife bought him a copy of the bestselling book, *The Magic of Thinking Big* by David J. Schwartz to encourage him.

This book suggests to write down everything you want to do before you die. So, Lou sat at his kitchen table and decided he was going to get out of his mental rut and start setting some big, audacious goals for his lifetime. He wrote 107 things he wanted to do. The list included:

- Be a guest on the The Tonight Show
- Coaching Notre Dame Football
- Meeting the Pope
- Have dinner at the White House
- Win a national championship

Holtz ended up achieving 102 of the 107 things he wrote. So write as big as you can from your heart. Don't let your mind tell you it's impossible. Just write whatever comes to you.

Habakkuk 2:2-3 has a framework on how to do this: "Write the vision and make it plain..."

So go get a journal and a pen. Sit quietly and prayerfully before the Lord and ask Him what does He have for your life.

I would encourage you to write 102 lifetime goals. It may sound like a lot, but this is your life we are talking about.

FOCUS ON TEN GOALS THIS YEAR

Now that you have your list of dreams, it is time to simplify what you want for this current year. Look at your list and choose ten goals you would like to accomplish. If you choose too many, it becomes harder to focus.

Brian Tracy says one of his favorite exercises is to imagine it is December 31st of this year, and as he looks back, he says, "This has been the most amazing year of my life."

What happened? What would make you leap with joy and say, "God... I can't believe You did that!"

Maybe it's:

- A new job
- Getting out of debt
- A dream vacation
- A new car
- Marriage
- A baby
- Starting your business
- Starting your ministry
- Getting to your healthiest weight
- Writing your book
- Going back to school
- Earning your certification or license
- Launching your website
- Saving $10,000

TURN DREAMS INTO SMART GOALS

God gives vision, but goals help you walk it out. Our goals give your dreams direction. It is one thing to say, "I want a better life." It is another thing to get specific and decide what that looks like. One tool that can help is creating **SMART goals**.

A SMART goal is a helpful tool used to guide goal setting. It is an acronym that stands for **Specific**, **Measurable**, **Achievable**, **Realistic**, and **Time-bound**. This method helps focus your efforts, create a clear plan, and increase your chances of achieving your goal.

Specific: Be clear about what you want.

Instead of saying, "I want more money," say, "I want to save $5,000."

Measurable: Track your progress.

What gets measured often gets improved. It also gives you something to celebrate along the way.

Achievable: Make it realistic and possible.

Big dreams are built through smaller daily steps.

Relevant: Choose goals that truly matter to your life and this season.

Not what looks good to others. What matters to you.

Time-bound: Give it a deadline.

A dream with a deadline becomes a goal.

Instead of saying, "One day I'll write a book," say, "I will finish my first draft by December 31st."

Did you ever notice that most productive day of the year is the year before a vacation. Or when someone is coming over to visit. Why? Because there is a timeline.

Write it down. Get clear. Put a date on it. Then begin.
Now that your goals are clear, let's put them where you can see them every day.

CREATE A VISION BOARD

Now that you have your list written. Go back and find up to ten things you want to accomplish this year. Pick goals for different areas of your life such as finances, health, hobbies, career, relationships, and travel.

Some things such as:

- Lose ten pounds
- Organize your closet.
- Brand new BMW.
- Family vacation to Disneyland.
- Earn $100,000.
- Earn your bachelor's degree.
- Write a best-selling book.
- Pay off a credit card for $5,000.
- Go on a missions trip to South Africa.

Now let's bring this to life. A vision board is more than arts and crafts. It is a visual reminder of where you are going and what you are believing God for. It keeps your dreams in front of you and helps you stay motivated, focused, and accountable.

Your vision board is a collage of images, words and symbols-representing your personal dreams and goals. As you begin to see those dreams come to pass one by one, it will build your faith, increase your confidence, and inspire you to keep dreaming bigger.

Most people think in pictures and images, not in words. When you think of a vacation, you don't spell out V-A-C-A-T-I-O-N, you see the place, the sun, them smell of the ocean. You are there in your mind. Since our mind responds strongly to visual stimulation (your goals and dreams in pictures), it is important that you see your dreams before.

You can be creative as you want. Search the internet for pictures, flip through your favorite magazines, find current pics of yourself. This is your future your dreaming up.

It can include areas where you want improvement, such as a credit score of 700, a spouse if you are single, new bedroom furniture, or a healthier lifestyle. It can also include desires like jewelry from Tiffany, new Nike shoes, or a new haircut. You can add goals such as "Top Sales Winner," "Best-Selling Author," or "Grammy Winner." It could also include your dream car or your apartment in Paris.

To create your board, gather supplies such as poster board, cork board, foam board, or even a notebook. You may want scissors, glue, tape, push pins, markers, stickers, glitter, paint, magazines, printed pictures, and inspirational quotes or scriptures. You can make it as creative or as simple as you would like.

Now give yourself a deadline, because a dream with a deadline becomes a goal. It is important to have big goals on the board, but you also need small obtainable goals as well.

SAMPLE GOALS

Goal #1: Pay of (specific name of card) Credit card of $1,000.

Print out a photo of a credit card. Then write on the photo or next to it: "Paid off credit card by April 22nd."

Goal 2: Become a Real Estate Agent.

Print out a photo of a real estate agent, a "Sold" sign, or homes you would like to sell. Research the cost of classes, exam fees, and licensing. Estimate your total goal cost. Then write this vision in plain sight: "Licensed Real Estate Agent by December 31st: $1,500."

Goal #3: Vacation in Australia.

Print out a photo of the resort you plan to stay at in Australia, places you want to visit. Research how much it would cost to achieve this goal. (Include travel, hotel, spending money, meals, tours, etc.): Write this vision "Vacation in Australia by December 31st: $12,000."

Goal #3: Run a half-marathon.

Print out a photo and find a picture of a person that ran the half-marathon and put your face on top of that. Also, find the metal you would win, cut that out and put it on the board. Find out how much it would cost to enter, clothes you need, etc. Then write in plain to see. I ran the half-marathon by July 31st.

Now that your board is complete, be sure to look at it every day. Act as if it has already come to pass. Thank God for it, and say out loud, "This is mine." Point to it. Lay hands on the photos if you would like. Speak over your goals in the present tense, as if they have already been achieved. Allow yourself to feel the joy, gratitude, and excitement of it already happening.

MY PARIS STORY: SEE IT BEFORE YOU SEE IT

In August 2017, my coworkers celebrated my birthday. When I returned to my desk, I looked at all the beautiful gifts they had given me, and so many of them had Paris imagery on them. Suddenly, I began to cry.

I had always wanted to see the Eiffel Tower in Paris and had dreamed of going there for years. I had even asked friends if they wanted to go with me, but they didn't. I sat there feeling the disappointment of that.

But while I sat at my desk, God whispered to my heart, "Stop waiting on other people to live your dreams."

When I got home that night, I found a picture of the Eiffel Tower and wrote on a piece of paper:

Paris, June 1–7, 2018

Then I placed it on my vision board.

I thought, I don't have the money or know how this will happen. But I put it on my vision board anyway.

And something happened when I put that vision in front of me. I got excited.

I started researching hotels, airports, and flights. I used Google Maps to "walk" the streets of Paris. I would zoom in on the Eiffel Tower and close my eyes, picturing myself standing right there in front of it, looking up at it and smiling.

I watched countless YouTube videos on the airport, the attractions, and how to get around. By the time I finally went, I had already visited Paris in my mind many times.

Then God began sending help. One of my brother's friends said, "If you create a GoFundMe page, I'll give toward your trip." He became my very first donor.

From there, 34 people gave toward my dream vacation. One person even said, "You're always serving others and doing God's work. Now we want to support you."

A volunteer at my job gave me videos all about Europe, a plug adapter, and helpful advice. She told me that most hotels in Paris speak English, and that helped me find a great hotel.

I got discounted flights and was even upgraded to what the airline called "business class."

And on May 31, 2018, I boarded that plane to Paris. I was there from May 31st to June 6th.

God did exactly what He whispered at my desk months earlier.

I put the vision before me, and God brought it to pass.

HOLD ON TO THE VISION

I once watched Steve Harvey share this story with the studio audience on Family Feud. He said that when he was in the sixth grade, he wrote on a paper, "I want to be on TV."

At the time, he had a severe stuttering problem and could barely speak. His teacher called him to the front of the class and humiliated him.

She asked, "Who in this school has ever been on TV? Who in your family has ever been on TV? Who in this neighborhood has ever been on TV?"

Then she said, "Look at you. You can't even talk. How are they going to put somebody like you on TV?"

But what she could not see was what God had already placed in his imagination.

Years later, after going through homelessness, losing everything, and facing setback after setback, he held on to that vision.

He said, "All I did was hang on to that thought. I just kept hoping. I just kept hoping that what I had written on that paper would come true. There were many times it wasn't even about faith. Sometimes I didn't believe it myself. When you're homeless and living in a car, how do you see yourself as a TV star? But I just kept hanging in there."

And today, you can hardly turn on the television without seeing him. He even said he sends that teacher a TV every year so she does not miss seeing him.

God did not give the dream to everyone else. He gave it to you.

You will have naysayers and people who do not believe you have what it takes. But this proves something: no one else has to believe in your dream for it to happen.

God did not give the dream to everyone else. He gave it to you.

So hold on to it until you see it come to pass.

KEEP MOVING FORWARD

You do not have to have everything figured out right now. You just need to take the next step. Start where you are, use what is in your hands, and trust what God has placed in your heart.

The same God who brought you through can also lead you forward.

REFLECTION QUESTIONS

1. What is one dream you still want to accomplish and why does it matter to you?
2. Who is one person that inspires you to dream bigger?
3. What is one small step you can take this week toward your dream?
4. What would your life look like one year from now if you stayed consistent?

COME AS YOU'LL BE FUN CHALLENGE

Jack Canfield shares a fun exercise that can energize your dreams, and I love the idea. He once hosted a "Come As You'll Be" party where everyone came dressed as the person they wanted to become five years later. They showed up as authors, successful business owners, wealthy professionals, speakers, and people living the lives they desired.

They brought props, talked about their accomplishments, celebrated their success, and acted as if it had already happened.

What made it so powerful is that, years later, many of them had actually become the very people they came dressed as. That is the power of vision. When you begin to see it, speak it, and move toward it, something starts to shift.

So why not try it for yourself?

Invite a few friends, family members, or coworkers and ask everyone to come as the person they will be five years from now after achieving their goals.

Come dressed as your future self. Bring props that represent your success, such as a book you wrote, business cards, travel photos, awards, keys to your dream car, or anything that matches the life you are believing for.

Then spend the evening celebrating. Talk about your accomplishments, how happy you are, how far you have come, and what God has done in your life. The key is that you cannot come out of your future self the entire night.

FAITH IS TAKING
THE FIRST STEP
EVEN WHEN YOU
DON'T SEE THE
WHOLE STAIRCASE.

- Martin Luther King Jr.

CONCLUSION: HOPE FOR CHANGE

I'M WRITING THIS ON A SIGNIFICANT DAY —THE SAME day this book began for me many years ago, on July 4th.

The day this country celebrates freedom.

But today, I'm celebrating something even more personal:

My freedom.

A day I once dreaded... is now a day I look forward to.

Years ago, on this very day, I didn't want to live.

I was overwhelmed, hopeless, and convinced my life had no way forward.

But God met me there.

He didn't just rescue me—He changed me.

And today, I am living proof of what He has done in my life. As a result, I am secure in Christ and in who He says I am. I have satisfying and fulfilling relationships, and I have healthy boundaries because I know how to say no and when to say yes without guilt. Because of that, I am no longer burnt out.

I charge my worth in business, and I take more chances in life. I have gotten better with rejection because I know it is not personal.

I'm still a work in progress, but I am excited about where I am going—and I never want to go back or look back.

When I began writing *I Understand: Discover Mental Health Wellness and Peace in Christ*, my goal was simple:

I wanted you to know you are not alone. It's okay to bring your pain, your questions, and even your weaknesses to God, and it's okay to lean on others who believe in His power to heal.

Because the truth is this:

Not only do I understand...God understands.

He sees every tear. He hears every silent prayer.

And He has already made a way for your healing, your peace, and your freedom in Christ.

And now, here we are—on this day of freedom—finishing what we started together.

A journey from surviving to thriving.

From despair to hope.

From brokenness to peace.

For years, I held on to a message from Joyce Meyer called "Hope for Change."

One line became my lifeline:

"I would rather hope for 100 percent and get 50 percent, than believe for nothing and get 100 percent of nothing."

That truth anchored me. Because hope is never wasted.

Even when change seems slow, even when nothing looks different yet.

Something is happening.

Pause and remember:

You didn't think you'd make it last year—but you did.

You didn't think you'd smile again—but you did.

You didn't think you'd bounce back—but you did.

The same God who carried you before is carrying you today.

His strength hasn't run out. His mercy hasn't expired. His plans for you haven't been canceled.

Proverbs 4:18 reminds us: "The path of the righteous is like the morning sun, shining ever brighter till the full light of day."

Your life is not growing dim; it's getting brighter!

Even now.

As I write this, fireworks are exploding outside. I'm missing the show, but somehow, I can see them in my mind. Each burst reminds me of God's faithfulness.

And in this moment, I'm reminded: Hope is still alive.

If you're ready to keep going, turn to the Mental Health Wellness Toolbox that follows. It is filled with scriptures, affirmations, and practical tools to help you walk out the life you desire, maintain your peace, and continue living free in Christ.

PRAYER OF SALVATION

If you want to know the same God who has brought me mental health wellness and peace in Christ, you can receive Him now.

The Bible says in Romans 10:9–10 that if you declare with your mouth, "Jesus is Lord," and believe in your heart that God raised Him from the dead, you will be saved. For it is with your heart that you believe and are justified, and it is with your mouth that you profess your faith and are saved.

So say this prayer out loud:

I believe that Your only begotten Son, Jesus Christ, shed His precious blood on the cross at Calvary and died for my sins, and I am now willing to turn from my sins. Father, I confess Jesus as the Lord of my life. With my heart, I believe that God raised Jesus from the dead. This very moment, I accept Jesus Christ as my personal Savior, and according to His Word, right now I am saved.

MENTAL HEALTH WELLNESS TOOLBOX

This section brings together many of the tools shared throughout the book, including diagrams, journal prompts, worksheets, and a quick reference guide. These resources are here so you can return to them whenever you need encouragement, clarity, or a reminder of the truth you've learned.

These resources are here to help you continue renewing your mind, strengthening your faith, and walking in peace, hope, and wholeness.

WHAT YOU WILL FIND IN THIS SECTION:

- Quick Reference Guide: When You Need Help Right Now Scriptures, Affirmations from Scriptures, and Prayers
- Ongoing Support
- Journal Exercise
- Recommended Books
- Research and Source Notes

QUICK REFERENCE GUIDE:
WHEN YOU NEED HELP RIGHT NOW

If you need encouragement in the moment, use this guide to go straight to the scriptures, affirmations, and prayers in the back of the book.

Go to the section that matches what you are facing right now and find God's Word, peace, and a way to move forward.

- In despair/at the end of yourself → Purpose & Surrender............183
- Hopeless → Hope............186
- Fearful, anxious, or stressed → Peace............189
- Overwhelmed, overcommitted, or drained → Healthy boundaries......192
- Angry, hurt, bitter, or struggling to forgive → Forgiveness............195
- Lonely or surrounded by the wrong people → Right relationships.....198
- Rejected or feeling not good enough → Accepted............201
- Unworthy or struggling with self-worth → Identity in Christ............203
- Neglected, abandoned, or betrayed → Loved............206
- Doubting God, yourself, or your future → Truth............209
- Negative, critical, or defeated by your words → Life-giving words....212
- Distracted or pulled away from God's best → Focus............216
- Lost or unsure of your future → Direction & Vision............219
- Afraid of settling or afraid of success → Courageous living........222

SCRIPTURES, AFFIRMATIONS, AND PRAYERS

This section is here to help you in the moment.
Read the scriptures.
Speak the affirmations until you believe them.
Pray the prayers.

As you read, speak, and pray, let your heart and mind come into agreement with what God says about you.

IN DESPAIR/AT THE END OF YOURSELF → PURPOSE/ SURRENDER

BE REMINDED THAT EVEN WHEN LIFE FEELS UNBEARABLE, GOD OFFERS RESTORATION AND NEW BEGINNINGS.

Trust in the Lord with all your heart; do not depend on your own understanding. Seek his will in all you do, and he will show you which path to take (Proverbs 3:5–6).

Commit everything you do to the Lord. Trust him, and he will help you (Psalm 37:5).

Commit your actions to the Lord, and your plans will succeed (Proverbs 16:3).

Give your bodies to God because of all he has done for you. Let them be a living and holy sacrifice—the kind he will find acceptable (Romans 12:1).

If any of you wants to be my follower, you must give up your own way, take up your cross, and follow me (Matthew 16:24).

So humble yourselves before God. Resist the devil, and he will flee from you (James 4:7).

My old self has been crucified with Christ. It is no longer I who live, but Christ lives in me (Galatians 2:20).

Humble yourselves under the mighty power of God, and at the right time he will lift you up in honor. Give all your worries and cares to God, for he cares about you (1 Peter 5:6–7).

Father, if you are willing, please take this cup of suffering away from me. Yet I want your will to be done, not mine (Luke 22:42).

PURPOSE & SURRENDER AFFIRMATIONS FROM SCRIPTURE

I trust in the Lord with all my heart. I do not depend on my own understanding. As I seek His will, He shows me the path I should take (Proverbs 3:5–6).

I commit everything I do to the Lord. As I trust Him, He helps me (Psalm 37:5).

I commit my actions to the Lord, and He establishes my plans (Proverbs 16:3).

I offer my life to God as a living sacrifice, holy and pleasing to Him (Romans 12:1).

I choose to follow Jesus. I lay down my own way and walk in His (Matthew 16:24).

I humble myself before God and resist the enemy. Through God's power, the enemy must flee (James 4:7).

My old life has been crucified with Christ. It is no longer I who live, but Christ who lives in me (Galatians 2:20).

I humble myself under God's mighty hand. I give all my worries and cares to Him because He cares for me (1 Peter 5:6–7).

Not my will, but God's will be done in my life (Luke 22:42).

PRAYER FOR PURPOSE & SURRENDER

Lord,

When I feel overwhelmed, exhausted, or at the end of myself, remind me that I do not have to carry everything alone. Help me surrender my plans, my fears, and my struggles to You. Teach me to trust You with all my heart and not rely on my own understanding. I commit my life, my decisions, and my future into Your hands. When I feel weak, remind me that Your strength is enough. Help me to humble myself before You and release every worry, knowing that You care deeply for me.

Today I choose to follow You. Not my will, but Your will be done in my life. Lead me, guide me, and restore my hope as I walk in the purpose You have for me.

In Jesus' name, amen.

HOPELESS → HOPE

FIND HOPE SCRIPTURES, AFFIRMATIONS, AND PRAYERS TO REMIND YOU THAT YOUR STORY ISN'T OVER.

But I will keep on hoping for your help (Psalm 71:14).

For I know the plans I have for you,' says the Lord. 'They are plans for good and not for disaster, to give you a future and a hope' (Jeremiah 29:11).

I pray that God, the source of hope, will fill you completely with joy and peace because you trust in him. Then you will overflow with confident hope through the power of the Holy Spirit (Romans 15:13).

The Lord is close to the brokenhearted; he rescues those whose spirits are crushed (Psalm 34:18).

Yet I still dare to hope when I remember this: The faithful love of the Lord never ends! His mercies never cease. Great is his faithfulness; his mercies begin afresh each morning (Lamentations 3:21–23).

Let us hold tightly without wavering to the hope we affirm, for God can be trusted to keep his promise (Hebrews 10:23).

Why am I discouraged? Why is my heart so sad? I will put my hope in God! I will praise him again—my Savior and my God! (Psalm 42:11).

But those who trust in the Lord will find new strength. They will soar high on wings like eagles (Isaiah 40:31).

HOPE AFFIRMATIONS FROM SCRIPTURE

I will keep hoping in God and trusting Him for help (Psalm 71:14).

God has good plans for my life. He is giving me a future and a hope (Jeremiah 29:11).

God, the source of hope, is filling me with joy and peace as I trust Him. I overflow with confident hope through the power of the Holy Spirit (Romans 15:13).

The Lord is close to me when my heart is broken. He rescues me when my spirit feels crushed (Psalm 34:18).

God's faithful love never ends. His mercies never cease. His mercies are new for me every morning (Lamentations 3:21–23).

I hold tightly to the hope I believe in, because God can be trusted to keep His promises (Hebrews 10:23).

When my heart feels discouraged, I will put my hope in God. I will praise Him again, my Savior and my God (Psalm 42:11).

As I trust in the Lord, He renews my strength. He lifts me up and helps me rise again (Isaiah 40:31).

PRAYER FOR HOPE

Lord,

When my heart feels heavy and my mind feels overwhelmed, remind me that my hope is in You. Thank You for being close to me when I am brokenhearted and for renewing Your mercy every morning. Help me to trust Your plans for my life, even when I cannot see the whole picture.

Fill my heart with Your peace and joy and strengthen me through Your Spirit. When discouragement tries to take hold of me, help me lift my eyes to You again. Renew my strength, restore my hope, and remind me that my story is not over because You are still writing it.

In Jesus' name, Amen.

FEARFUL, ANXIOUS, STRESSED → PEACE

TURN TO SCRIPTURES AND AFFIRMATIONS THAT CALM YOUR HEART AND QUIET ANXIOUS THOUGHTS.

You will keep in perfect peace those whose minds are steadfast, because they trust in you (Isaiah 26:3).

Do not let your hearts be troubled. You believe in God (John 14:1).

Peace I leave with you; my peace I give you. I do not give to you as the world gives. Do not let your hearts be troubled and do not be afraid (John 14:27).

Do not be anxious about anything, but in every situation, by prayer and petition, with thanksgiving, present your requests to God. And the peace of God, which surpasses all understanding, will guard your hearts and your minds in Christ Jesus (Philippians 4:6–7).

You will keep in perfect peace those whose minds are steadfast, because they trust in you (Isaiah 26:3).

The Lord gives strength to his people; the Lord blesses his people with peace (Psalm 29:11).

Let the peace of Christ rule in your hearts (Colossians 3:15).

May the God of hope fill you with all joy and peace as you trust in him (Romans 15:13).

Now may the Lord of peace himself give you peace at all times and in every way (2 Thessalonians 3:16).

PEACE AFFIRMATIONS FROM SCRIPTURE

As I trust in the Lord, He keeps my mind in perfect peace (Isaiah 26:3).

I will not let my heart be troubled. I trust in God (John 14:1).

Jesus has given me His peace. I do not have to live in fear or anxiety (John 14:27).

I bring my worries and concerns to God in prayer. His peace, which is beyond my understanding, guards my heart and mind in Christ Jesus (Philippians 4:6–7).

The Lord gives me strength and blesses me with peace (Psalm 29:11).

The peace of Christ rules in my heart and guides my thoughts (Colossians 3:15).

As I trust in God, He fills me with joy and peace, and my hope grows stronger through the power of the Holy Spirit (Romans 15:13).

The Lord of peace gives me peace at all times and in every situation (2 Thessalonians 3:16).

PRAYER FOR PEACE

Lord,

When fear and anxiety begin to overwhelm my mind, help me remember that Your peace is available to me. Teach me to bring every worry and concern to You in prayer instead of carrying it on my own. Calm my heart and quiet my thoughts. Help me trust You fully, knowing that You are in control even when life feels uncertain. Let Your peace guard my heart and mind so that fear no longer has power over me.

Fill me with Your strength, Your presence, and Your peace that surpasses all understanding. I choose to trust You and rest in the peace You give.

In Jesus' name, Amen.

OVERWHELMED, OVER-COMMITTED, OR DRAINED → HEALTHY BOUNDARIES

FIND WISDOM TO PROTECT YOUR PEACE AND CREATE HEALTHY LIMITS.

But let your 'Yes' be 'Yes,' and your 'No,' be 'No.' For whatever is more than these is from the evil one (Matthew 5:37).

So let each one give as he purposes in his heart, not grudgingly or of necessity; for God loves a cheerful giver (2 Corinthians 9:7).

The fear of man is a trap, but I put my trust in the Lord and I am kept safe (Proverbs 29:25).

Am I now seeking the approval of man or of God? Or am I trying to please man? If I were trying to please man, I would not be a servant of Christ (Galatians 1:10).

I am a messenger of God who has been entrusted with the gospel. My purpose is not to please people, but God who examines my heart and motives (1 Thessalonians 2:4).

Everybody wants to make friends with the ruler, but my judgment comes from the Lord (Proverbs 29:26).

I work willingly and wholeheartedly because I work for God and not man. I know that it is the Lord that rewards me for my efforts because my service is solely to Christ (Colossians 3:23–24).

Promotion comes neither from the east, west, or south. But God is the judge: He decides who will rise and who will fall (Psalm 75:6–7).

HEALTHY BOUNDARIES AFFIRMATIONS FROM SCRIPTURE

My words are clear and honest. My yes means yes, and my no means no (Matthew 5:37).

I give freely and cheerfully, not out of pressure or obligation (2 Corinthians 9:7).

I do not live in fear of people's opinions. I trust the Lord, and He keeps me safe (Proverbs 29:25).

I seek God's approval above all else, not the approval of people (Galatians 1:10).

I live to please God, who knows my heart and my motives (1 Thessalonians 2:4).

I trust God with the outcome of my life, because my direction and judgment come from Him (Proverbs 29:26).

I work wholeheartedly for the Lord and not for people. My reward comes from Him (Colossians 3:23–24).

My promotion and advancement come from God alone (Psalm 75:6–7).

PRAYER FOR HEALTHY BOUNDARIES

Lord,

When I feel overwhelmed, over-committed, or pressured to please everyone, help me remember that my life belongs to You. Give me wisdom to set healthy boundaries and the courage to say no when necessary.

Help me seek Your approval above the approval of others. Teach me to trust that my purpose, promotion, and provision come from You, not from trying to satisfy everyone around me.

Give me discernment to know when to say yes and when to say no. Help me give and serve from a willing and cheerful heart, not out of guilt or pressure.

Protect my peace and guide my decisions so that I live in balance, wisdom, and obedience to You.

In Jesus' name, amen.

ANGRY, HURT, BITTER, OR STRUGGLING TO FORGIVE → FORGIVENESS

LEARN HOW FORGIVENESS FREES YOUR HEART AND RESTORES PEACE.

If you forgive those who sin against you, your heavenly Father will forgive you. But if you refuse to forgive others, your Father will not forgive your sins (Matthew 6:14–15).

Make allowance for each other's faults and forgive anyone who offends you. Remember, the Lord forgave you, so you must forgive others (Colossians 3:13).

Get rid of all bitterness, rage, anger, harsh words, and slander, as well as all types of evil behavior. Instead, be kind to each other, tenderhearted, forgiving one another, just as God through Christ has forgiven you (Ephesians 4:31–32).

But when you are praying, first forgive anyone you are holding a grudge against, so that your Father in heaven will forgive your sins too (Mark 11:25).

Do not judge others, and you will not be judged. Do not condemn others, or it will all come back against you. Forgive others, and you will be forgiven (Luke 6:37).

He has removed our sins as far from us as the east is from the west (Psalm 103:12).

If we confess our sins to him, he is faithful and just to forgive us our sins and to cleanse us from all wickedness (1 John 1:9).

Come now, let's settle this, says the Lord. Though your sins are like scarlet, I will make them as white as snow (Isaiah 1:18).

Love prospers when a fault is forgiven, but dwelling on it separates close friends (Proverbs 17:9).

FORGIVENESS AFFIRMATIONS FROM SCRIPTURE

I choose to forgive others just as God has forgiven me (Matthew 6:14–15).

I make room for others' mistakes and release offenses from my heart (Colossians 3:13).

I let go of bitterness, anger, and harsh words. I choose kindness, compassion, and forgiveness (Ephesians 4:31–32).

When I pray, I release every grudge and forgive those who have hurt me (Mark 11:25).

I refuse to judge or condemn others. I choose forgiveness and freedom (Luke 6:37).

God has removed my sins as far as the east is from the west, and I extend that same grace to others (Psalm 103:12).

When I confess my sins, God is faithful to forgive me and cleanse me completely (1 John 1:9).

God restores and cleanses my heart, making what was once stained pure again (Isaiah 1:18).

When I forgive, love grows and relationships can be restored (Proverbs 17:9).

PRAYER FOR FORGIVENESS

Lord,

You know the hurts I carry and the pain that sometimes makes it difficult to forgive. Help me release every offense, every grudge, and every bitterness that has taken root in my heart.

Teach me to forgive the way You forgive—freely and with grace. Remind me that forgiveness is not about excusing the wrong, but about freeing my heart from the weight of anger and resentment. Heal the places in my heart that have been wounded. Fill me with Your compassion and help me extend the same mercy You have shown me.

Today I choose forgiveness. I release the past into Your hands and allow Your peace to take its place.

In Jesus' name, Amen.

LONELY OR SURROUNDED BY THE WRONG PEOPLE → RIGHT RELATIONSHIPS

BE REMINDED THAT GOD DESIGNED US FOR HEALTHY RELATIONSHIPS AND SUPPORT.

My innermost circle will only be those whom I know are pure and godly. They will be the only ones I allow to minister to me (Psalm 101:6).

I have sweet friendships that refresh the soul and awaken my heart with joy, for good friends are like the anointing oil that yields the fragrant incense of God's presence (Proverbs 27:9).

Walk with the wise and become wise; associate with fools and get in trouble (Proverbs 13:20).

As iron sharpens iron, so a friend sharpens a friend (Proverbs 27:17).

Don't be fooled by those who say such things, for bad company corrupts good character (1 Corinthians 15:33).

Always be humble and gentle. Be patient with each other, making allowance for each other's faults because of your love (Ephesians 4:2).

Since God chose you to be the holy people he loves, you must clothe yourselves with tenderhearted mercy, kindness, humility, gentleness, and patience. Make allowance for each other's faults and forgive anyone who offends you (Colossians 3:12–13).

Do all that you can to live in peace with everyone (Romans 12:18).

Two people are better off than one, for they can help each other succeed. If one person falls, the other can reach out and help (Ecclesiastes 4:9–10).

A friend is always loyal, and a brother is born to help in time of need (Proverbs 17:17).

A man that hath friends must show himself friendly, and there is a friend that sticketh closer than a brother (Proverbs 18:24).

RIGHT RELATIONSHIPS AFFIRMATIONS FROM SCRIPTURE

I choose to surround myself with people who are honest, pure, and walk with God. (Psalm 101:6)

My I choose to surround myself with people who are honest, pure, and walk with God (Psalm 101:6).

My friendships refresh my soul and bring joy to my heart (Proverbs 27:9).

As I walk with wise people, I grow in wisdom and understanding (Proverbs 13:20).

Healthy friendships sharpen me and help me grow into the person God created me to be (Proverbs 27:17).

I choose relationships that strengthen my character and encourage my faith (1 Corinthians 15:33).

I treat others with humility, gentleness, patience, and love (Ephesians 4:2).

I clothe myself with kindness, mercy, humility, and patience as I build healthy relationships (Colossians 3:12–13).

I do everything I can to live in peace with others (Romans 12:18).

God places supportive people in my life who help me succeed and lift me up when I fall (Ecclesiastes 4:9–10).

I am blessed with loyal friendships that support me in times of need (Proverbs 17:17).

I show myself to be friendly, and I build meaningful relationships. I am surrounded by genuine connections, and I have a friend who sticks closer than a brother (Proverbs 18:24).

PRAYER FOR RIGHT RELATIONSHIPS

Lord,

Thank You for creating us to live in relationship with others. When I feel lonely or surrounded by the wrong influences, guide me toward healthy relationships that strengthen my faith and bring encouragement to my life.

Help me choose friendships that reflect wisdom, kindness, and integrity. Give me discernment to recognize relationships that build me up and the courage to step away from those that lead me away from Your best.

Teach me to be the kind of friend who shows humility, patience, love, and grace. Surround me with people who encourage me, sharpen me, and help me grow in my walk with You.

Thank You for placing the right people in my life at the right time.

In Jesus' name, amen.

REJECTED OR FEELING NOT GOOD ENOUGH → ACCEPTED

DISCOVER THE COURAGE TO RISE ABOVE REJECTION AND WALK CONFIDENTLY IN WHO GOD CREATED YOU TO BE.

Even before he made the world, God loved us and chose us in Christ to be holy and without fault in his eyes. God decided in advance to adopt us into his own family by bringing us to himself through Jesus Christ (Ephesians 1:4–5 NLT).

He has made us accepted in the Beloved (Ephesians 1:6).

Thank you for making me so wonderfully complex! Your workmanship is marvelous—how well I know it (Psalm 139:14).

You are precious to me. You are honored, and I love you (Isaiah 43:4).

You received God's Spirit when He adopted you as His own children (Romans 8:15).

You are a chosen people, a royal priesthood, a holy nation, God's very own possession (1 Peter 2:9).

Nothing can ever separate us from God's love (Romans 8:38–39).

ACCEPTED AFFIRMATIONS FROM SCRIPTURE

God loved me and chose me even before the world was created. I belong to Him (Ephesians 1:4–5).

I am accepted in Christ and welcomed into God's family (Ephesians 1:6).

I am wonderfully made by God. His workmanship in my life is marvelous (Psalm 139:14).

I am precious to God. I am honored, and I am loved (Isaiah 43:4).

I have been adopted into God's family through His Spirit. I am His child (Romans 8:15).

I am chosen by God. I am part of His royal priesthood and His special possession (1 Peter 2:9).

Nothing can separate me from the love of God (Romans 8:38–39).

PRAYER FOR ACCEPTANCE

Lord,

When feelings of rejection or insecurity try to take hold of my heart, remind me of who I am in You. Thank You for loving me, choosing me, and adopting me into Your family.

Help me see myself the way You see me—valuable, chosen, and deeply loved. When the voices of doubt or past rejection try to define me, strengthen my heart with Your truth.

Teach me to walk confidently in the identity You have given me. Let Your love quiet every fear and heal every place where rejection once lived. Remind me that nothing can separate me from Your love.

In Jesus' name, amen.

UNWORTHY OR STRUGGLING WITH LOW SELF-WORTH → IDENTITY IN CHRIST

REDISCOVER YOUR WORTH AND VALUE THROUGH GOD'S PERSPECTIVE.

For we are God's masterpiece. He has created us anew in Christ Jesus, so we can do the good things he planned for us long ago (Ephesians 2:10).

You are a chosen people. You are royal priests, a holy nation, God's very own possession (1 Peter 2:9).

Even before he made the world, God loved us and chose us in Christ to be holy and without fault in his eyes (Ephesians 1:4).

His Spirit joins with our spirit to affirm that we are God's children (Romans 8:16).

Anyone who belongs to Christ has become a new person. The old life is gone; a new life has begun (2 Corinthians 5:17).

Thank you for making me so wonderfully complex! Your workmanship is marvelous—how well I know it (Psalm 139:14).

For you are all children of God through faith in Christ Jesus (Galatians 3:26).

So, you also are complete through your union with Christ (Colossians 2:10).

IDENTITY IN CHRIST AFFIRMATIONS FROM SCRIPTURE

I am God's masterpiece. He created me in Christ for a purpose and good works prepared just for me (Ephesians 2:10).

I am chosen by God. I belong to Him and am part of His royal family (1 Peter 2:9).

God loved me and chose me even before the world was created (Ephesians 1:4).

God's Spirit confirms that I am His child. I belong to Him (Romans 8:16).

Because I belong to Christ, I am a new person. My old life is gone, and my new life has begun (2 Corinthians 5:17).

I am wonderfully made by God. His workmanship in my life is marvelous (Psalm 139:14).

Through faith in Christ, I am a child of God (Galatians 3:26).

I am complete in Christ (Colossians 2:10).

PRAYER FOR IDENTITY IN CHRIST

Lord,

When I struggle with feelings of unworthiness or doubt my value, remind me of who I am in You. Help me see myself through Your eyes and not through the lies of insecurity or comparison.
Thank You for creating me with purpose and calling me Your own. Thank You for choosing me, loving me, and making me new through Christ. Help me walk confidently in the identity You have given me.

Replace every negative thought about myself with Your truth. Remind me that I am Your child, Your masterpiece, and that my life has meaning and purpose in You.

In Jesus' name, Amen.

NEGLECTED, ABANDONMENT, BETRAYED → LOVED

MEDITATE ON THE PROMISES THAT GOD WILL NEVER LEAVE YOU NOR FORSAKE, NO MATTER WHAT YOU HAVE DONE IN LIFE.

Can anything ever separate us from Christ's love? Does it mean he no longer loves us if we have trouble or calamity, or are persecuted, or hungry, or destitute, or in danger, or threatened with death? (As the Scriptures say, "For your sake we are killed every day; we are being slaughtered like sheep. No, despite all these things, overwhelming victory is ours through Christ, who loved us. And I am convinced that nothing can ever separate us from God's love. Neither death nor life, neither angels nor demons,[b] neither our fears for today nor our worries about tomorrow—not even the powers of hell can separate us from God's love. No power in the sky above or in the earth below—indeed, nothing in all creation will ever be able to separate us from the love of God that is revealed in Christ Jesus our Lord (Romans 8:35, 37-39).

For God so loved the world, that he gave his only begotten Son, that whosoever believeth in him should not perish, but have everlasting life (John 3:16).

Love suffers long and is kind; love does not envy; love does not parade itself, is not puffed up; does not behave rudely, does not seek its own, is not provoked, thinks no evil; does not rejoice in iniquity, but rejoices in the truth; bears all things, believes all things, hopes all things, endures all things. Love never fails (1 Corinthians 13:4-8).

There is no fear in love. But perfect love drives out fear, because fear has to do with punishment. The one who fears is not made perfect in love (I John 4:18).

Let all that you do be done in love (1 Corinthians 16:14).

Above all, love each other deeply, because love covers over a multitude of sins (1 Peter 4:8).

May the Lord make your love increase and overflow for each other (1 Thessalonians 3:12) .

LOVE AFFIRMATIONS FROM SCRIPTURE

Nothing can separate me from Christ's love. Trouble, hardship, persecution, lack, danger, or fear do not mean I am unloved. In all these things, I have overwhelming victory through Christ who loves me. I am convinced that nothing in all creation—can ever separate me from the love of God that is in Christ Jesus (Romans 8:35, 37–39).

God so loved me that He gave His only Son for me. Because I believe in Him, I will not perish but have everlasting life (John 3:16).

I walk in love, that is patient and kind. I do not envy, boast, or act in pride. I do not behave rudely or seek my own way. I am not easily angered, and I choose not to hold on to wrongs. I rejoice in truth. I bear all things, believe all things, hope in all things, and endure all things. Love in my life never fails (1 Corinthians 13:4–8).

God's perfect love drives out fear in my life. I do not live in fear, because I am being made complete in His love (1 John 4:18).

Everything I do is done in love (1 Corinthians 16:14).

I love others deeply, and love in my life covers faults and brings healing (1 Peter 4:8).

The Lord is increasing my love and causing it to overflow toward others (1 Thessalonians 3:12).

PRAYER FOR LOVE

Father,

Thank You that You are love, and because You live in me, I have the ability to love. I bow my heart before You and choose to believe the best about others and the best about myself.

Teach me to love my neighbor as myself—with patience, kindness, and grace. Help me release negative thoughts, comparison, and doubt, and replace them with Your truth.

When I feel discouraged or tempted to give up, remind me that Your love never fails. Strengthen me to keep going, to keep growing, and to keep walking in love.

Fill my heart with Your love so that it overflows into every relationship and every area of my life. Let my words, my thoughts, and my actions reflect who You are.

Thank You that I am loved, secure, and never alone.

In Jesus' name, Amen.

DOUBTING GOD, YOURSELF, OR YOUR FUTURE → TRUTH

RENEW YOUR MIND WITH TRUTH THAT REPLACES DOUBT AND STRENGTHENS YOUR FAITH.

You will know the truth, and the truth will set you free (John 8:32).

God is not a man, so he does not lie. He is not human, so he does not change his mind. Has he ever spoken and failed to act? Has he ever promised and not carried it through? (Numbers 23:19)

My thoughts are nothing like your thoughts, says the Lord. And my ways are far beyond anything you could imagine. (Isaiah 55:8–9) But blessed are those who trust in the Lord and have made the Lord their hope and confidence (Jeremiah 17:7).

Let us hold tightly without wavering to the hope we affirm, for God can be trusted to keep his promise (Hebrews 10:23).

For we live by believing and not by seeing (2 Corinthians 5:7).

For the word of the Lord holds true, and we can trust everything he does (Psalm 33:4).

For all of God's promises have been fulfilled in Christ with a resounding Yes (2 Corinthians 1:20).

TRUTH AFFIRMATIONS FROM SCRIPTURE

As I know God's truth, it sets me free (John 8:32).

God does not lie or change His mind. What He promises, He always fulfills (Numbers 23:19).

God's thoughts and ways are higher than mine. I trust His wisdom even when I do not understand (Isaiah 55:8–9).

I am blessed because I trust in the Lord. He is my hope and my confidence (Jeremiah 17:7).

I hold tightly to the hope I believe in, knowing God always keeps His promises (Hebrews 10:23).

I live by faith and trust in God, even when I cannot see the full picture (2 Corinthians 5:7)

The word of the Lord is true, and everything He does is trustworthy (Psalm 33:4).

All of God's promises are fulfilled in Christ. His answer over my life is Yes (2 Corinthians 1:20).

PRAYER FOR TRUTH

Lord,

When doubt fills my mind and I question You, myself, or my future, remind me of Your truth. Help me to replace every lie with what Your Word says about me and about my life.

Strengthen my faith so that I trust Your promises even when I cannot see the outcome. Teach me to walk by faith and not by sight. When my thoughts become overwhelmed with uncertainty, guide me back to Your truth that never changes.

Thank You that Your Word is trustworthy and that every promise You make is faithful and true. Help me hold tightly to hope and believe what You say about my life.

In Jesus' name, amen.

NEGATIVE, CRITICAL, OR DEFEATED BY YOUR WORDS → LIFE-GIVING WORDS

LEARN HOW SPEAKING DIFFERENTLY CAN SHIFT YOUR MINDSET AND BRING ENCOURAGEMENT.

The tongue can bring death or life; those who love to talk will reap the consequences (Proverbs 18:21).

Indeed, we all make many mistakes. For if we could control our tongues, we would be perfect and could also control ourselves (James 3:2).

Gracious words are a honeycomb, sweet to the soul and healing to the bones (Proverbs 16:24).

For out of the abundance of the heart the mouth speaks. A good man out of the good treasure of his heart brings forth good things, and an evil man out of the evil treasure brings forth evil things. But I say to you that for every idle word men may speak, they will give account of it in the day of judgment. For by your words you will be justified, and by your words you will be condemned (Matthew 12:34,35, & 37).

The words of the reckless pierce like swords, but the tongue of the wise brings healing (Proverbs 12:18).

A gentle answer turns away wrath, but a harsh word stirs up anger (Proverbs 15:1).

The soothing tongue is a tree of life, but a perverse tongue crushes the spirit (Proverbs 15:4).

Do not let any unwholesome talk come out of your mouths, but only what is helpful for building others up according to their needs (Ephesians 4:29).

Let your conversation be always full of grace, seasoned with salt (Colossians 4:6).

May the words of my mouth and the meditation of my heart be pleasing in your sight, Lord (Psalm 19:14).

Set a guard over my mouth, Lord; keep watch over the door of my lips (Psalm 141:3).

I love life and I see good days; therefore, I refrain my tongue from evil and my lips from speaking deceit (1 Peter 3:10).

There is a time for me to keep silent and there is a time for me to speak (Ecclesiastes 3:7).

A [shortsighted] fool always loses his temper and displays his anger, but a wise man [uses self-control and] holds it back (Proverbs 29:11).

LIFE-GIVING WORDS AFFIRMATIONS FROM SCRIPTURE

My words bring life and encouragement. I choose to speak words that build up and not tear down (Proverbs 18:21).

With God's help, I am learning to control my tongue and my responses (James 3:2).

My words are gracious, bringing sweetness to the soul and healing to the heart (Proverbs 16:24).

What fills my heart produces good words. I choose to fill my heart with truth, faith, and encouragement (Matthew 12:34–35, 37).

My words bring healing rather than harm. I speak with wisdom and kindness (Proverbs 12:18).

My gentle words bring peace and calm to situations (Proverbs 15:1).

My tongue is a tree of life that encourages and strengthens others (Proverbs 15:4).

I speak words that build others up and meet their needs (Ephesians 4:29).

My conversations are full of grace and wisdom (Colossians 4:6).

The words of my mouth and the thoughts of my heart are pleasing to the Lord (Psalm 19:14).

God places a guard over my mouth and watches over my words (Psalm 141:3).

I choose words that lead to life and blessing (1 Peter 3:10).

I have wisdom to know when to speak and when to remain silent (Ecclesiastes 3:7).

I practice self-control and choose wisdom over anger (Proverbs 29:11).

PRAYER FOR LIFE-GIVING WORDS

Lord,

Help me become more aware of the words I speak. When negativity, criticism, or discouragement tries to come out of my mouth, remind me of the power my words carry.

Teach me to speak with wisdom, kindness, and grace. Help my words bring healing, encouragement, and life to others. Guard my mouth and guide my heart so that what I say reflects Your truth and love.

When I feel angry or frustrated, give me self-control and wisdom to pause before I speak. Fill my heart with Your peace so that my words reflect the goodness inside.

May the words of my mouth and the meditation of my heart always be pleasing to You.

In Jesus' name, amen.

DISTRACTED OR PULLED AWAY FROM GOD'S BEST → FOCUS

REFOCUS YOUR HEART AND MIND ON WHAT TRULY MATTERS.

Today I have given you the choice between life and death, between blessings and curses. Now I call on heaven and earth to witness the choice you make. Oh, that you would choose life, so that you and your descendants might live! (Deuteronomy 30:19)

We do this by keeping our eyes on Jesus, the champion who initiates and perfects our faith (Hebrews 12:2).

Think about the things of heaven, not the things of earth (Colossians 3:2).

Seek the Kingdom of God above all else, and live righteously, and he will give you everything you need (Matthew 6:33).

I will study your commandments and reflect on your ways (Psalm 119:15).

Look straight ahead and fix your eyes on what lies before you. Mark out a straight path for your feet; stay on the safe path (Proverbs 4:25–26).

You will keep in perfect peace all who trust in you, all whose thoughts are fixed on you (Isaiah 26:3).

FOCUS AFFIRMATIONS FROM SCRIPTURE

I choose life and the path that leads to God's blessings (Deuteronomy 30:19).

I keep my eyes on Jesus, the author and finisher of my faith (Hebrews 12:2).

My mind is focused on things above and not distracted by temporary things (Colossians 3:2).

I seek God's kingdom first, and He provides everything I need (Matthew 6:33).

I study God's Word and reflect on His ways (Psalm 119:15).

My eyes look straight ahead, and I walk confidently on the path God has set before me (Proverbs 4:25–26).

As I fix my thoughts on God and trust Him, He fills me with perfect peace (Isaiah 26:3).

PRAYER FOR FOCUS

Lord,

When my mind becomes distracted and my attention drifts away from what truly matters, help me refocus on You. Remind me that my purpose and direction are found in keeping my eyes on Jesus. Help me choose the path that leads to life, wisdom, and peace. Guide my thoughts so they remain centered on Your truth instead of the distractions around me. Teach me to seek Your kingdom first and trust that You will provide everything I need.

Give me clarity, discipline, and peace as I walk forward in the path You have set before me. Help me stay focused on what matters most and live a life that honors You.

In Jesus' name, Amen.

LOST OR UNSURE OF YOUR FUTURE → DIRECTION

GAIN CLARITY AND ENCOURAGEMENT FOR THE PATH AHEAD.

For I know the plans I have for you," says the Lord. "They are plans for good and not for disaster, to give you a future and a hope (Jeremiah 29:11).

I glorified you on earth by completing down to the last detail what you assigned me to do (John 17:4).

The Lord directs our steps, so why try to understand everything along the way? (Proverbs 20:24)

Our God, will you not judge them? For we have no power to face this vast army that is attacking us. We do not know what to do, but our eyes are on you (2 Chronicles 20:12).

Trust in the Lord with all your heart; do not depend on your own understanding. Seek his will in all you do, and he will show you which path to take (Proverbs 3:5-6).

I will instruct you and teach you in the way you should go; I will counsel you with my loving eye on you (Psalm 32:8).

Whether you turn to the right or to the left, your ears will hear a voice behind you saying, 'This is the way; walk in it.' (Isaiah 30:21)

The Lord directs the steps of the godly. He delights in every detail of their lives (Psalm 37:23–24).

If any of you lacks wisdom, let him ask of God, who gives generously to all without reproach, and it will be given to him (James 1:5).

DIRECTION AFFIRMATIONS FROM SCRIPTURE

God has good plans for my life. He is giving me a future and a hope (Jeremiah 29:11).

God has given my life purpose, and I will walk in the assignments He has prepared for me (John 17:4).

The Lord directs my steps, even when I do not understand every part of the journey (Proverbs 20:24).

When I do not know what to do, I fix my eyes on God and trust Him to lead me (2 Chronicles 20:12).

I trust in the Lord with all my heart and do not rely on my own understanding. As I seek His will, He shows me the path I should take (Proverbs 3:5–6).

God instructs me and teaches me the way I should go. His loving eye is guiding me (Psalm 32:8).

God speaks to my heart and shows me the way to walk (Isaiah 30:21).

The Lord directs my steps and cares about every detail of my life (Psalm 37:23–24).

When I need wisdom, I ask God and He generously gives it to me (James 1:5).

PRAYER FOR DIRECTION

Lord,

When I feel uncertain about my future or unsure of the next step, remind me that You are guiding my path. Help me trust that Your plans for my life are good and filled with hope.

Teach me to rely on Your wisdom instead of my own understanding. When I feel confused or overwhelmed, help me pause and fix my eyes on You. Lead me step by step and give me the courage to follow where You guide.

Thank You for directing my life with love and care. I trust that You are working in every detail of my journey.

In Jesus' name, Amen.

AFRAID OF SETTLING OR AFRAID OF SUCCESS → COURAGEOUS

GIVE YOURSELF PERMISSION TO STEP INTO THE LIFE GOD HAS PREPARED FOR YOU.

We are confident of all this because of our great trust in God through Christ. It is not that we think we are qualified to do anything on our own. Our qualification comes from God (2 Corinthians 3:4-5).

He who began a good work in you will carry it on to completion until the day of Christ Jesus (Philippians 1:6).

Have I not commanded you? Be strong and courageous. Do not be afraid; do not be discouraged, for the Lord your God will be with you wherever you go (Joshua 1:9).

For God has not given us a spirit of fear, but of power and of love and of a sound mind (2 Timothy 1:7).

So do not throw away your confidence; it will be richly rewarded. You need to persevere so that when you have done the will of God, you will receive what he has promised (Hebrews 10:35–36).

So do not fear, for I am with you; do not be dismayed, for I am your God. I will strengthen you and help you; I will uphold you with my righteous right hand (Isaiah 41:10).

The Lord is my light and my salvation—whom shall I fear? The Lord is the stronghold of my life—of whom shall I be afraid? (Psalm 27:1) Be strong and courageous. Do not be afraid or terrified because of them, for the Lord your God goes with you; he will never leave you nor forsake you (Deuteronomy 31:6).

Be on your guard; stand firm in the faith; be courageous; be strong (1 Corinthians 16:13).

If God is for us, who can be against us? (Romans 8:31)

COURAGE AFFIRMATIONS FROM SCRIPTURE

My confidence comes from my trust in God through Christ. My qualification and ability comes from Him (2 Corinthians 3:4–5).

God began a good work in me, and He will faithfully complete it (Philippians 1:6).

I am strong and courageous. I will not be afraid or discouraged, because the Lord my God is with me wherever I go (Joshua 1:9).

God has not given me a spirit of fear, but of power, love, and a sound mind (2 Timothy 1:7).

I will not throw away my confidence. As I persevere in doing God's will, I will receive what He has promised (Hebrews 10:35–36).

I will not fear, because God is with me. He strengthens me, helps me, and upholds me (Isaiah 41:10).

The Lord is my light and my salvation, so I have nothing to fear (Psalm 27:1).

I am strong and courageous because the Lord goes with me and will never leave me nor forsake me (Deuteronomy 31:6).

I stand firm in my faith. I am courageous and strong (1 Corinthians 16:13).

Because God is for me, nothing can stand against me (Romans 8:31).

PRAYER FOR COURAGE

Lord,

When fear tries to keep me small or convince me that I am not capable, remind me that my strength and confidence come from You. Help me release the fear of settling for less than what You have prepared for me, and also the fear of stepping into the calling You have placed on my life.

Fill me with courage, wisdom, and boldness to move forward in faith. When doubt whispers that I am not enough, remind me that You are the one who equips me and completes the work You began in me.

Help me stand firm, trust Your promises, and walk confidently in the life You have prepared for me.

In Jesus' name, Amen

YOUR ONGOING SUPPORT

For additional tools, encouragement, and guided exercises, visit: **www.erickagloriousmoore.com/resources**.

You'll find:

- Encouragement videos
- Affirmations
- Downloadable tools
- Practical next steps
- Videos where I personally encourage and coach you through key exercises from this book.
- Spoken affirmations you can declare aloud to strengthen faith, peace, and confidence.
- Downloadable worksheets and activity guides to help you apply what you've learned.

Whenever you feel stuck or need a reminder, this is your safe place to return.

JOURNAL EXERCISE: THE 5-MINUTE RESET

(Referenced from Memoirs of Singlehood and the Steps Toward Marriage)

This exercise helps you separate feelings from facts and recognize thought patterns.

How it works:

1. Set a timer for five minutes.
2. Write freely — no editing, no filtering.
3. Include:
    - The good (what's working)
    - The bad (what hurts or frustrates you)
    - The ugly (honest thoughts you usually hide)

Then:

4. Go back and highlight thoughts that do NOT align with God's Word.
5. Replace each one with a scripture.
6. Meditate on those scriptures throughout the day.
7. Now you are ready to fight the good fight of faith for the day.

This practice trains you to recognize mental patterns and renew your mind intentionally.

RECOMMENDED BOOKS

These resources helped shape the journey shared in this book:

The Bible (Daily foundation)

Boundaries — Dr. Henry Cloud & Dr. John Townsend

What to Say When You Talk to Yourself — Shad Helmstetter

Exchanging Your Thoughts for God's Thoughts — Dr. Robb Thompson

Zero Victim — Pastor James Ward

Winning the War in Your Mind — Craig Groeschel

Dream It, Pin It, Win It — Terri Savelle Foy

RESEARCH

Throughout this book, references are made to widely recognized findings in psychology, neuroscience, and behavioral research.

These include:

1. The brain's release of dopamine in response to reward and progress (motivation and habit reinforcement)
2. The concept of neuroplasticity—the brain's ability to rewire through repeated thought patterns and behaviors
3. Research on social influence and habits, including studies published in the New England Journal of Medicine
4. Insights into workplace success and relational intelligence from the Harvard Business Review
5. Health and relationship findings from organizations such as the Mayo Clinic and the American Psychological Association

SOURCE NOTES

Chapter 3
Ward, James. Zero Victim. 2014

Chapter 4
https://www.centerforbibleengagement.org/post/bible-engagement-a-key-to-spiritual-growth

https://cedwardpitt.com/2014/01/29/dr-caroline-leaf-and-the-98-percent-myth/

https://www.facebook.com/share/r/1Dw2kUXFFE/

Chapter 5
Hankins, Mark. Never Run at Your Giant with Your Mouth Shut! 2001 Pg 22

Mehl, Matthias R., et al. "Are Women Really More Talkative Than Men?" Science, 317(5834), 2007.

Brysbaert, Marc, et al. "How Many Words Do We Know? Practical Estimates of Vocabulary Size..." Frontiers in Psychology, 2016.

Oxford English Dictionary, vocabulary statistics.

National Center for Voice and Speech, speaking rate research summaries.

Helmstetter, Shad. What to Say When You Talk to Yourself. Pocket Books, 1986.

Fredrickson, Barbara L., and Marcial Losada. "Positive Affect and the Complex Dynamics of Human Flourishing." American Psychologist, 2005.

Savelle Foy, Terri. If It's Not the Way You Want It, Stop Saying It. YouTube video. https://youtu.be/HMicOuoruA8

Chapter 6
Harrington, Jananya. "5 Benefits Gratitude Has on the Brain." Holy Culture. https://holyculture.net/read/artlcle/5-benefits-gratitude-has-on-the-brain

Seligman, M. E. P., Steen, T. A., Park, N., & Peterson, C. (2005). Positive Psychology Progress: Empirical Validation of Interventions. American Psychologist, 60(5), 410–421.

Chapter 7
Allen, Jennie. Find Your People: Building Deep Community in a Lonely World. WaterBrook, 2022, p. 54.

Chapter 8
Shetty, Jay. https://www.facebook.com/jayshetty/posts/they-say-the-human-mind-has-around-60000-thoughts-every-single-day-and-nearly-80/1439435224209727/

Chapter 9
American Institute of Stress. "What the Latest Reports Say About

Chapter 10
Stress in America." Stress.org. Accessed April 19, 2026. https://www.stress.org/news/what-the-latest-reports-say-about-stress-in-america/

Mayo Clinic Staff. "Friendships: Enrich Your Life and Improve Your Health." Mayo Clinic. Accessed April 19, 2026. https://www.mayoclinic.org/healthy-lifestyle/adult-health/in-depth/friendships/art-20044860

Chapter 12
https://www.smithsonianmag.com/innovation/7-epic-fails-brought-to-you-by-the-genius-mind-of-thomas-edison

Chapter 13
Canfield, Jack. The Success Principles: How to Get from Where You Are to Where You Want to Be. New York: HarperCollins, 2005. Chapter 1, "Take 100% Responsibility for Your Life."

Chapter 14
Foy, Terry Savelle. Dream It. Pin It. Live It. 2015, p. 3.

https://www.linkedin.com/pulse/act-host-come-you-party-prof-pravat-mahapatra/

https://www.huffpost.com/entry/lou-holtzs-compelling-que_b_794675

OVERCOMER

ABOUT THE AUTHOR

Ericka Glorious Moore is a high-energy, interactive motivational speaker, best-selling author, mental health coach, and entrepreneur dedicated to helping people release their past, thrive in the present, and walk confidently into their future. She is known for her relatable, engaging, and faith-centered approach, using research, laughter, and personal experience to equip people with the tools they need to heal, grow, and excel.

For over a decade, Ericka has inspired audiences through workshops, presentations, and community events, sharing her personal journey of overcoming adversity—including bullying, loss, depression, and thoughts of suicide—to become a voice of hope and transformation. Her message is simple yet powerful: no matter what you've been through, you can overcome and create a life filled with purpose and peace.

Ericka empowers people to shift their mindset, establish healthy boundaries, and take ownership of their lives so they can walk boldly in who God created them to be. Through her speaking, coaching, and writing, she provides practical strategies that lead to real, lasting change.

In addition to her work in personal development, Ericka is also an award-winning designer and entrepreneur, blending creativity and strategy to help brands and individuals communicate their stories effectively. Whether on stage, online, or through her books, her mission remains the same: to help people break free from limiting beliefs, know their value, and discover their dreams.

OTHER BOOKS BY ERICKA GLORIOUS MOORE

Discover Memoirs of Singlehood and the Steps Toward Marriage, available in paperback and eBook.

For more information, please visit:

erickagloriousmoore.com

Available wherever books and eBooks are sold.

ADDITIONAL RESOURCES

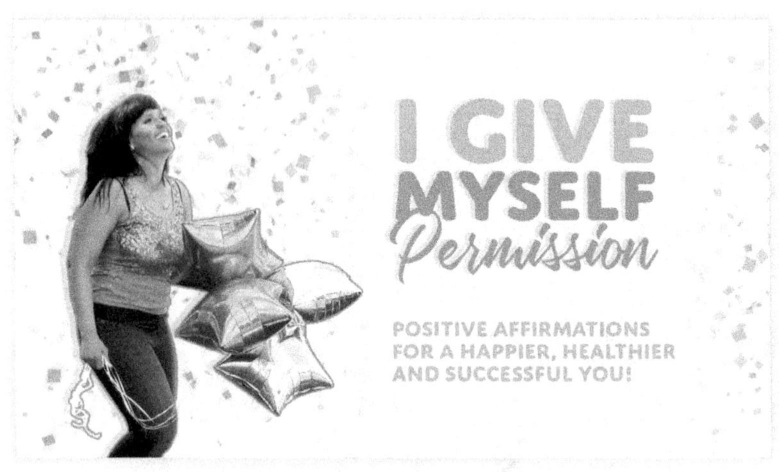

Unlock Happiness, Health, and Success with
"I Give Myself Permission" Affirmations
(Includes MP3 and accompanied affirmations sheet)

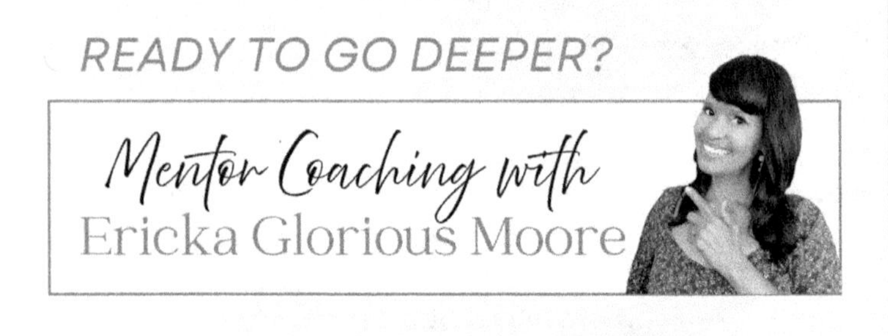

Take the next step in your journey with personalized coaching designed to help you break free from limiting beliefs, know your value, and discover your dreams.

To learn more, please visit:

erickagloriousmoore.com

STAY CONNECTED

SUBSCRIBE TO MY YOUTUBE CHANNEL

Facebook
@erickagloriousmoore

Instagram
@erickagloriousmoore

YouTube
@erickagloriousmoore

Website
www.erickagloriousmoore.com

Join My Newsletter
www.erickagloriousmoore.com/emails

"Know Your Value, Discover Your Dreams"

www.ingramcontent.com/pod-product-compliance
Lightning Source LLC
LaVergne TN
LVHW050620100826
845148LV00011B/1664

* 9 7 9 8 2 3 4 0 5 7 1 2 9 *